Hiding My Bruises While Singing In the Choir
My Personal Hallmark® Movie

By:
Jan Juliano Balzer

Editors:
Teresa Marbut
Dennis Lugo-Coll

Cover Design:
Jay Niemeyer
Jeff Johnson

Author's Photo:
Amy West

Copyright © 2011

ISBN# 978-1-4507-9480-0

Dedication

This book is dedicated to my husband, Doug Balzer, and to my two children, Jaylene Johnson and Jeremy Balzer, and to my mother, Edrea Juliano

Doug

You are my hero, knight in shining armor, counselor, best friend, and husband. Your commitment to me is so deeply rooted in love; you have endured so many things on our journey. Thank you for standing by me and for always being patient, loving, and understanding. Thank you for teaching me so many things - I can't even begin to list them all - but especially for teaching me how to love again. You have led our family well; you are a fantastic father and grandfather. I am in awe every day of the love and commitment you have for me. I love you with all of my heart and will cherish you all of my days.

Jaylene

You are my blue eyed, blond hair, life changing miracle. You took my world by storm and held me together through some of the most difficult circumstances. You were my reason for living and making a conscious decision to do better. And all that before you were even one year old. Today, you are still my hero. I am so proud of who you've become; a loving wife, a tremendous mother of four, and my friend. Your grace and strength amaze me. Thank you for your forgiveness, love, and understanding. I hold you dear to my heart and love you more than you will ever know. (Thank you also for the four amazing grandchildren!)

Jeremy

You are my brown eyed, brown hair baby boy who the minute you were born I knew you would be a journey all its own. *(You know what I'm talking about!)* You have become an amazing young man; full of life. You have a tender heart and have so much talent to offer the world. I believe God has amazing plans for you. You have overcome so many things in your life. I'm proud of your accomplishments. You have brought so much joy and fun into my life. Thank you for the grace and forgiveness you have shown to me despite being raised by someone (me) with PSTD. Always remember my love for you is unconditional and forever.

Mom

You are always there for me and for my family. You have loved me, guided me, helped me, and prayed for me my whole life. You have been my steadfast rock of stability. Your support has helped me endure so many things I had to walk through. You've stood by me no matter what and showed grace and kindness when they were not deserved. Thank you for your wisdom, friendship, and unconditional love. You are an amazing lady and have blessed so many people in your lifetime. I will always treasure you; I love you deeply.

Acknowledgments

Kathleen (Wegeleben) Powell
We met in 1971 and were instantly best friends. You play a huge part in my life! The majority of my childhood memories include you. We grew up singing together, confiding in each other, laughing, crying, encouraging, supporting, and loving each other like true sisters. Today, we still carry that bond of sisterhood and friendship. I am honored to call you my best friend.

Venus Maria (Reams) Braning
You have been my friend, roommate, and match maker who introduced me to Doug. We have walked through so much together and our friendship is holding stronger than ever. Thank you for your strength, faith, love, and encouragement over all the years. You are dear to my heart.

Teresa Marbut and Dennis Lugo-Coll
Teresa, you talked me down out of many trees during this process. Dennis, your expertise in the literary world has been such a blessing. Thank you both for taking an interest in this project and being the best and most patient editors there are.

Jay Niemeyer and Jeff Johnson
Jay, your artwork is exquisite and I'm honored to be featuring your work on my book cover. Jeff, you say, "easy peasy" – but for most of us, what you do is not easy at all. Thank you both for sharing your talent with me for this book cover. I think it's amazing.

Gina (Frigeri) Parris
Your encouragement and advice has been so greatly appreciated. Thank you for letting me hang out with you in Tennessee to get this project started. I consider you one of my mentors. Thank you for leading by example and speaking life into so many people.

Frank and Debbie Juliano, and, Linda, Clarence and Louise Seely
Thank you for being my safe haven when I needed to travel to Spokane to get away from all the crazy things going on in my life. Your hospitality and love will never be forgotten. I love and treasure you all.

Lori (Fenner) Pallister and Mary Fenner
Thank you for taking me and my baby in during the most crucial time in my life. Because of your generosity and support, I was able to escape a horrible situation and get back on my own two feet. I will forever be grateful to you both.

Marsha (Williams) Cramer
You drove over with your truck more times than I can count to help me move out – only to help me move back home again a day or two later. Thank you for your friendship and help. You will always have a special place in my heart.

Dawn Juliano
You always had my back; making sure I had cash and food and helping me in every little way you possible could. I am moved by your generosity and will always remember the love and support you gave me. I love you dear sister.

Contents

Introduction 5

Prologue 6

Section One – An overview of my journey

1   Once Upon A Time . . . 11

2   Pulling Up Roots 15

3   College Bound 21

4   My Dreams Would Have to Wait 25

5   Road Trip with a Newborn 29

6   The Rent Race 39

7   Doug Who? 42

8   God Sent Me a Guardian Angel 46

9   I Do 59

10   Full Circle 62

Section Two – Scenes that played out

11   Another Confirmation Please, I Didn't Like the First One 66

12   Choir Robes Don't Hide Black Eyes 74

13   That Darned Volkswagen 83

14   Dear Prozac, Thank You! 93

15   All My Clothes Are Shrinking 104

16   I Like Happy Endings, Don't You? 111

Section Three – Insights, Facts, and Resources

17   Our Perception is Our Reality 114

18   Shattered Photographs 125

19   Why Don't You Just Leave? 132

20   Facts about Domestic Violence 135

21   Resources for: 138

    Domestic Violence

    Teen Pregnancy/Abortion

    Cancer

    Suicide

    Substance Abuse

    Alcohol Abuse

Introduction

When I look at my life in story form, it hardly seems real. It actually reminds me of one of those Hallmark movie channel movies. It certainly has all the makings for one. There's romance, drama, death due to diseases, abuse (both mental and physical), abortion, drugs, alcohol, and suicide. All the while, I'm still singing in the choir, bruises and all. It's not the most "fuzzy" feeling story most of the time, but, the ending isn't so bad. Through lots of struggle, depression, anger, and finally submitting my broken pieces to God, hope, healing, joy, and "normal" happened. Whatever "normal" is.

For every bad adventure, there has been a good adventure. For every devastating event, there has been redemption by God that is so amazing no one could imagine. Through every struggle and difficult time, God has been right there at my side protecting me and giving me peace and comfort. This book, *Hiding my Bruises While Singing in the Choir,* will take you through parts of my journey in the hopes that it will help you find your own redemption and peace from whatever life has brought your way. My intent is for you to see my story and relate it to your own. To show you God's redeeming power and to give you hope that there is "normal"—whatever normal is—after the "traumatic". Through my quirky humor that is housed within my own brokenness, I hope that you find your own happy ending to your life's journey.

Prologue
In Loving Memory of Nathan G. Skiller
May 1964 – Oct 1983

In October, 1983, my world was turned upside down & inside out. In all of these years since, there isn't one day that has gone by that I haven't remembered, wondered, mourned, laughed, cried, felt angry, felt sad, or struggled to allow myself to be happy and to live a normal life. Truly, my world has never been the same and the path that I have walked has not been easy, but is our path ever easy?

My story is your typical, "I married my high school sweetheart" story. Or, at least it started out that way. Girl meets Boy. Girl likes Boy. Boy likes Girl... We were soul mates. It was supposed to be one of those stories that the grandkids would admire and find hope in. Where the "Once upon a time" actually had a "they lived happily ever after." But instead of all it should have been, in the land of fairy tales, this story lands in the "tragedy/drama" category rather than the "romance/comedy" one. *(I personally prefer the romantic comedy movies to the thrillers or dramatic ones).*

We've always been told that the choices we make all throughout our lives are extremely important. As teens in high school, we think we have all the answers. Our lives are mapped out just so, and we imagine exactly how life will look as we get older. We have no realization of the obstacles and challenges that are out there waiting for us. We don't understand that every step we take is laying the foundation of who we will become. And we *absolutely* don't imagine that anything bad or tragic would even enter into our world.

When I am with my grandchildren, watching my daughter, or just enjoying something simple in life, my heart is so sad and heavy. I often find myself thinking, "Nathan would have so enjoyed seeing this." My heart breaks. The story of Nathan and I and the tragedy that was our marriage is what you will find amongst these pages. But, that is not the entire story of my life, and you will find that, as well. You see, I walk a fine line of grieving my past and living my present. Yet, even in the midst of that, I know that God has redeemed me and blessed me tremendously! My life has been restored and I am living the "Once upon a time / happily ever after" story. But there are days that I feel guilty for being happy. While I know there is no guilt or shame in living the redeemed life, I am still very affected by the events of twenty-seven years ago.

The eleven months that I was married to Nathan were some of the most horrifying moments of my life. While the first five months were on track to be something great, the last six months had nothing but "bad movie" written all over them. I didn't learn this until six or seven years later, but it all started to go sour the night a friend returned home from boot camp for the Army. He wanted to take Nathan to a movie, but instead of the movie, Nathan was re-introduced to drugs. Until this person confessed to me what really happened that night, I had no idea what caused such a drastic turn in Nathan's life.

We met in the middle of my junior year when my family and I moved to Silverton, OR. For us, it was an instant connection. I think we were a "couple" within my first month at the new school. Over the years, I have had to learn how to shift my thoughts and memories to the good ones of those years and not focus on the six months that went so horribly wrong. Not an easy task, but over time, I have managed to pull the memories of who Nathan really was and not the Nathan he became under the influence of drugs and alcohol. I choose to remember the two years of bliss rather than the six months of horror.

Nobody really knows or understands how or why someone could take his or her own life. When the empty field that was next to my apartment went up in flames, I still refused to believe that Nathan was ending his life; and yet, at the same time, I felt that my life was finally safe from harm. It was a horrible rampage of emotion. Mourning the one I loved, and yet thankful that the monster that lived in him would never hurt me again. The abuse would stop. He would never pick me up and throw me across the room again. The mental and emotional torture would cease. Perhaps I would even stop throwing-up every time I heard a Volkswagen drive up to my apartment.

Yes, in October, 1983, my life was turned upside down & inside out. And in all this time I have been trying to figure out what I'm supposed to do with all these pieces that I'm holding in my heart. Nevertheless, God has been so incredibly faithful to me. He has kept His protecting hand on my life and has replaced all that I lost.

But you just can't forget…

It's impossible to live as if nothing has ever happened. Yet, I know I'm here for a purpose. My heart goes out to others who are walking through traumatic things. I just want to wrap my arms around them and tell them, "It will all be okay." God is a good God. People sometimes suck. But always and forever, God is a redeeming God and He can take those pieces we hold and make them into beautiful works of art; it just requires that we let go and offer up all those disjointed pieces to be made whole again. He is a gentle God and will not pry them out of our hands, so we have to be willing to let go, and let God do what he does best – heal us.

I will forever remember Nathan as he was when he was whole. When we laughed and giggled, and played, and cried. Those piercing blue eyes and the brightest smile you could imagine. That is the Nathan I choose to hold close to my heart.

Nathan, I forgive you, and I miss you.
And please know that all is well.

Section One
An Overview of My Journey

Chapter 1

Once Upon a Time . . .

I have many "once upon a times" in my life story. I think we all do. Every new chapter in our life starts with this phrase. Unfortunately, not all of them end with "happily ever after." The good news is that while we may have to endure some detours and rocky roads, in the end, God can put our lives back on track and give us purpose.

Once upon a time, a little girl born in Spokane, WA (way back when) was filled with all sorts of dreams and aspirations. She had three other sisters and one brother. She loved being the baby of this half Italian and half Scotch-Irish family. She wanted nothing more than to be a wife and mother and at the age of seven, she heard the call of God to ministry. Specifically, she wanted to be a pastor's wife. Her life was happy. She felt secure and loved. Her parents sheltered her from the harmful ways of life and she was confident in every way. Church was her second home. Her mother was very active in serving in the church. Every time the doors were open, the little girl was there, often dragging half the neighborhood kids with her. Music was also especially important to this little girl. Her love of singing and playing the piano shined through her every time the opportunity arose for her to give a performance. For the first fifteen years of this young life, everything was perfect. There was a want for nothing, and friends were plentiful. The future was bright. In fact, she had it all planned out. She would have the most picture perfect family, two kids, a husband, a dog, and a cat. Her husband would be a pastor and the whole family would sing together. After high school graduation, she would attend Bible College where she would meet this said husband. Yes, the future was very bright, until one day.

This little girl was me. But I'm guessing you have already figured that out! I truly did feel like I had the perfect life. But as life would have it, my journey was about to get rougher.

At the age of fourteen, my family found out that my dad had liver cancer. By this time, all my older siblings were out of the house, in college, or married already. So my mom and I took on the brunt of the care for my dad, and it turned into a very stressful year of watching him deteriorate. But equally as painful was seeing the toll it took on my mom; it made my heart break.

As all the kids gathered for Christmas, we tried to make it as normal as possible, but dad was very sick, and couldn't even keep his food down. There were a lot of tears that December as we all came to the realization that this would be dad's last Christmas with us. Over the next couple of months, dad became almost a skeleton and as weak as a tiny babe. The dead weight of my dad was becoming more than my mom could handle. Yet, she mustered up every bit of her strength to help him physically, and often I had to help lift him because we needed to turn him every few hours in order to avoid bedsores.

Dad didn't want to use the bed pan; I think his pride was still a little strong. We Italians can be pretty stubborn. So, every day, mom and I would lift him out of the hospital bed that was set up in my old bedroom and onto the toilet chair that was next to the bed. I'm sure it was just as embarrassing for my dad, but mom and I would often tease him and try to make the best of the situation. Every once in awhile we'd see a grin on his face, but for the most part, he was in a lot of pain and I'm sure the experience was not pleasant for him. My mom is one tough cookie and has a reserve of fortitude unlike anyone I've ever seen, so the night she broke down in my arms I knew she was spent. Exhausted and growing weak herself, she had no more strength to continue the kind of care she had been giving to her husband, my dad. She wept in my arms as we stood at the foot of my father's deathbed. I whispered in her ear, "It's going to be okay."

That night, I crawled into my mom's bed to sleep. I wanted to be there with her so she would not be alone. As I lay on my pillow, I prayed, "Lord, it's time; please take my dad home tonight. He has suffered enough and my mom is exhausted. Please, Lord, I ask you. Take him home to be with you. Amen."

The next morning my mom came to wake me up. She kissed me on the check and said, "Dad's gone." I knew before she even told me. Somehow I knew God had answered my prayer.

"Thank you Lord," I whispered. "You are such a faithful and loving God. Thank you for answering my prayer."

Sometimes I feel guilty for praying that prayer. Who prays for death? It could even be that dad would have passed that night anyway. It may not have been my prayer that sent him home. Who's to say? It was my way of releasing him, I suppose. I was ready for my dad's passing. I had seen enough suffering and I wanted him to be whole in the presence of Jesus. It also showed me just how much Jesus cared for us by answering my prayer for relief. I knew where my father was and it was a much better place! I was fifteen and a sophomore in high school at the time of my dad's death. This was also my first time losing a loved one. My faith and my church family were very instrumental in bringing me through this experience. Knowing that my dad was in heaven brought me a lot of confidence and strength, which gave me the ability to move on with my own life. But sometimes our life lessons are just first steps in preparation for what is to come.

Chapter 2

Pulling Up Roots

Nine months after my father passed away, my grandfather fell ill. My grandparents lived in Silverton, OR, which is a small town North East of Salem. I was just beginning my Junior year in high school where I was very active in jazz choir and drama. When my mom announced that she had to go to Oregon to take care of grandpa, she asked if I would be willing to go with her. I was not too thrilled about this prospect, being that it was my Junior year and all. I didn't really want to spend my Senior year at a new high school where I didn't know anybody. I especially didn't want to give up my music and drama involvement. I couldn't very well send my mom down to Oregon alone to take care of grandpa though, so of course, I agreed to go with her. A year would most likely go by quickly and I could resume my life.

Mom went down a few weeks ahead of me and I joined her after my semester ended for Christmas break. Mom had already chosen a church to attend and had met quite a few of the youth that were there. They were awaiting my arrival and were very eager to meet me. My transition was flawless and I struck up many new friendships even before the winter term of school began by attending the youth functions at the new church. My new friend Debi and I had an instant connection. Once school started, Debi made me feel very welcomed and introduced me to teachers and other students. I was even able to get an impromptu audition with the music teacher for the jazz choir during one of my lunch hours. There weren't any openings, but other members of the choir convinced the music director to hear me out. Within my first few days of school, I had a great youth group to attend, tons of new friends, and a spot in the jazz choir! Perhaps this wasn't going to be such a bad year after all.

We were living with my grandparents. Our clothes and a few personal items were all we brought with us. Our one-year stay had stretched into two. Grandpa was still very ill and we were still needed to help take care of him. Mom and I rented our own home in the country during my Senior year. I was ok with the extended stay because I was having a blast. Our jazz choir took first in state and I was having a blast singing, acting, and hanging out with my new friends. Especially one particular friend; his name was Nathan. Debi introduced us on my very first day at the school. It didn't take us long at all to become a couple and start dating. One week to be exact. He stood over 6' tall, had bright brilliant blue eyes, brown hair, and a smile that didn't end. He was funny, caring, smart, and he was mine! When I say I made lots of new friends, I should mention that I also made a few enemies. Seems like a lot of girls had their eye on Nathan and when the new girl came to town and stole his heart, it didn't sit well with them. But nonetheless, we were soul mates and it was the most amazing relationship I have ever experienced up until that time in my life.

We attended youth group and church together and spent almost every waking moment doing things with our friends. My mom adored him. They had a great relationship as well. Everything just felt right; perfect.

Nathan and I were extremely close and as happens all too often in these types of relationships, we entered into a sexual relationship a year after we started dating. We walked through the typical drama of narrow escapes with pregnancy and feeling the guilt and shame of having sex. Nathan decided to break up with me because we couldn't gain control over this area in our relationship. It was the only way he felt we would stop having sex. My heart was broken and crushed. I cried endlessly every day for weeks; mourning our lost relationship. All the plans and dreams we had together just smashed to the ground.

We were broken up for most of our Senior year of high school. During this time, Nathan returned to using drugs and drinking. (He used drugs and alcohol prior to us meeting.) He figured I wouldn't want anything to do with him if he was messed-up in that sort of stuff. He had this mindset that things were either black or white. There were never any in-between areas. No grey areas. He was either whole-heartedly on fire for God or entrenched in the party life. Once a mistake was made, that was it; no asking for forgiveness and moving on from there. He was swinging on the other end of the pendulum.

I had this idea that if Nathan could just hear me sing at the annual talent show at the high school, he would run back into my arms and everything would be how it was supposed to be. I selected the most beautiful song that expressed exactly how I felt about Nathan. I put a dedication to him in the program even. "Somewhere down the road" was the name of the song by Barry Manilow. It was perfect because it talked about how sometime, some place, our lives would cross again and we would realize that we belonged together. But he didn't show up that night. I was once again heartbroken.

When it was time for the Senior Prom I was very sad. We often talked about Senior Prom; we had so much fun at our Junior Prom. It felt so odd being at the Prom with someone else; someone that I hardly new and only liked as a friend.

Graduation was just around the corner. All the plans Nathan and I had talked about were now just broken dreams lying at my feet. We were going to go to Bible College together and get married one day. He wanted to be a youth pastor. At the graduation ceremony, we locked eyes for a brief moment and I saw that great smile one more time. I know he was thinking, "We did it! We're graduating!" I had a glimmer of hope that things might be okay after graduation. But then he quickly snapped back into reality and looked away – never to talk to me or look at me the rest of the night.

Shortly after graduation, my grandfather passed away. It was hard walking through that without my best friend by my side. I longed for his comfort and being held in his arms. Nathan always made me feel safe.

A couple weeks later I was home alone when I saw Nathan's car pulling into our driveway. My heart jumped up into my throat and I couldn't believe my eyes. Why was he coming over? Was he going to ask me to get back together? When he came to the door, he was very melancholy. I could see that he was unhappy. As we sat on the front lawn and talked, I remembered the song I had sung at the talent show. I asked him to come inside so I could sing him a song that I had dedicated to him. He sat by me on the piano bench and as I started to play and sing, tears began to flow down his face. By the time I was through singing, we both were crying and he held me in his arms. He then told me that he had impure intentions for coming over that day. He was hoping we would have sex again because he missed me so much that he felt that it was futile being apart. After hearing me sing to him, he realized sex wasn't the answer, though. Giving his heart back to God was. We talked a little while longer and decided to drive over to my grandma's house where my mom was visiting.

When we arrived at my grandma's house, my mom was very surprised to see Nathan with me. They embraced in a long hug and again, tears started streaming down all of our faces. We all sat at the kitchen table and mom and Nathan talked for what seemed to be hours. It was so good to see that their relationship was taking up right where it had left off. I excused myself to go use the little girl's room. When I came back to the table, mom asked Nathan if he wanted to share his good news with me, or if he wanted her to share. Nathan began to share with me how while I was in the bathroom they prayed together and he gave his heart back to God. Again, tears flowed and celebration was in the air. Then I thought to myself, "Wow, how long was I in the bathroom? I always miss the good stuff!"

Nathan and I talked for days about getting back together. We wanted to be together for the right reasons and not get caught up in our old pattern of having sex.

After a couple of weeks, Nathan and I were back together as a couple again and our plans and dreams were coming back to life. I would soon be heading off to Eugene to attend Bible College so we made the best of every moment. Nathan didn't have the funds to enroll for the Fall term so he planned to stay in Silverton and work. We worked hard to stick in groups and do things with other people so we wouldn't have any physical temptations. It was a good effort and we almost succeeded. In my last week prior to moving to Eugene, we started to realize that we would be apart for long periods of time. We became inseparable as we counted the months we would be apart. In a moment of weakness, we gave in as a way to say goodbye to each other. We had sex one more time. I left for Eugene a few days later.

Chapter 3

College Bound

Eugene Bible College had been part of my life since I was in first grade. The college at that time was affiliated with the church I grew up in and I knew my whole life that EBC was the college I wanted to attend. Choirs and drama groups' traveled through the area during the summers ministering and promoting the college. They were often at our youth camps as well. Yes, EBC was the place for me. I had a couple scholarships too, one from EBC for a music contest I had won my Senior year in high school; and one from the local Kiwanis Club in Silverton, OR.

Since I was attending college in Eugene, Oregon, mom decided to stay put and not return home to Spokane. For some reason the thought of being an hour and a half away rather than ten hours away was very appealing to her . . . and to me. So, she moved to Salem and rented a house there. Nathan decided to enroll in a Certified Nurse's Aide program in Salem. He moved in with my mom and started his classes. Mom was even helping him pay his tuition. It was good to see that things were starting to fall back into place and the life we established in Oregon wasn't so bad after all.

Dorm life was amazing! I finally made it to EBC. I was one of the first two freshmen to audition for a premier singing group, Zammar, and I made it that year!! This group was normally reserved for Juniors and Seniors only. It was a big deal! Two Freshmen made it, and one of them was me. I couldn't believe it! I was now going to be in one of the groups that traveled all summer and helped at youth camps. I had amazing floor mates, bathroom buddies, and a great roommate. College life was awesome.

Not too long after the term began, things got a little crazy. Nathan showed up every weekend to visit, and on the weekends he couldn't come to Eugene, he insisted on me coming home. When he was on campus with me, he was very possessive and got irritated when I talked with other guys. He started scolding me and telling me who I could talk with and who I couldn't talk with. Basically, if it was a girl, it was okay to engage. Jealousy started to rise up within him and I had no idea why or what prompted it. He was no longer happy that I was moving forward with my dreams. It became more about him and how he was being left behind. Some of my friends started to notice his behavior and began to question what was happening. Some felt it was unhealthy that I didn't have a weekend that didn't include seeing him. I felt the same way, so I started to do more things with my college friends on the weekends. Nathan didn't like this, but it was the right thing to do.

Meanwhile, I was having a blast singing in Zammar. Rehearsals were exhilarating and I felt so blessed being part of this group. At that time, the group only had eight singers. We had an awesome ensemble. When the time finally came for our first performance, we all piled into the van and traveled to a small country church not too far away. This was the moment I had been dreaming about my whole life! The performance was great and we got to talk with lots of the youth afterwards. On the way home, I began to feel very car sick. I had never felt car sick before. I'm the one who rides the hammer head at all the amusement parks. I told the driver to pull over, and that I wasn't feeling too well. He pulled over; I got out and stood at the side of the road puking.

The next morning when I woke up, I still didn't feel well. I spent a considerable amount of time in the bathroom throwing up some more. There was a flu bug going around campus and I must have caught it. So I thought. Every morning for weeks, I would get up and immediately run to the bathroom to throw up. The rest of the day I was fine. I made it to classes and rehearsals without being sick. It seemed to be just a morning thing. Day-by-day as this kept up, it began to sink in . . . I was pregnant. I set-up a doctor's appointment and continued my normal routine as best I could, since I had to wait a few days for my appointment.

My doctor's appointment confirmed my self-diagnosis. I would have been very surprised if I hadn't been pregnant. I called Nathan to tell him the news. We discussed how we were going to tell my mom and decided that he would tell her since he was living with her. We felt she should be told in person. I, however, had to let the Dean of Students know my situation. After days and days of avoiding what had to be done, I finally mustered up enough nerve to knock on the office door of the Dean. She could tell by my face that I had something heavy on my heart.

"I don't know how to say this any other way so here it goes. I'm pregnant." As I said those words, I began to cry. I braced myself for what she would say to me in return. I knew I would have to leave the school. I knew there would be great disappointment and perhaps judgment. Instead, I was embraced with a hug of compassion and kind words of assurance that everything was going to be all right. Her offer to me was incredible. I would be allowed to remain and finish out the term since I would still not be showing a "pregnant belly." It was late September just after mid-terms. I could leave for the remaining school year when the winter term began and return the following school year. She gave me the option of thinking about it, or if I wanted to leave sooner, I could. I told her I wanted to go home, so we called my mom and asked her to come get me. As I began to pack up my dorm room, I had to start explaining to my friends why I was leaving. We shared many hugs and lots of tears as we said our goodbyes. I was crushed over the fact I would have to leave Zammar. This had been my life-long dream; attending EBC and singing in a traveling group. But now it was all slipping right through my fingers.

Chapter 4

My Dreams Would Have to Wait

My mom allowed both of us to live with her in Salem. We really didn't have any other options at the time. Nathan was still in school and I was pregnant. We had a November wedding planned. My mom was gracious and threw us the whole meal deal! The wedding was beautiful and intimate. All of our friends and family were there to offer support and love. Shortly after the wedding, mom decided that Oregon was pretty much our permanent home now, so she sold our house in Spokane and bought a house in Salem. We all moved into the new spacious home together and awaited and planned for the arrival of our baby.

Nathan still exuded some behaviors that made me very uncomfortable. He was jealous of anyone I talked to, especially if they were male. He told me what I could and couldn't eat or when I had to sleep and what I could wear. He began to correct my speech; if I mispronounced a word, he would get in my face and make me repeat it over and over again until I got it right and not in a nice way, either. He made me feel so stupid and I started questioning if I had made the right decision to marry him.

During one of his outbreaks, Nathan picked up one of the formal dining room chairs and threw it at my mom. The chair did not hit her, but it was enough to get him kicked out of her house - immediately. In my mind, I was thinking about how much I wanted to stay with my mom, but Nathan was my husband and I felt I had to go with him. So, I gave my mom a hug and we drove out the driveway. My stomach felt like it was in my throat. We had no clue where we were going to sleep that night. I was in my ninth month of pregnancy, the end of May. We drove to his parent's house in the Silverton Hills. His parents said we could stay there up until the baby was born. There wasn't enough room in their single wide trailer for all the baby things and a small family. Nathan's grandparents lived in Silverton, as well, so they agreed to let us stay with them after the baby was born. So it was all lined out. We'd stay with his parents until I gave birth, and then go to his grandparent's house until we could get our own apartment. That gave me a little bit of security, but it was not how I had envisioned things would be. Giving birth to my first born was supposed to be an exciting, glorious time in life.

Nathan was working his internship at a Nursing Home in Salem. He worked a swing shift, which put him home very late at night. One weekend, Nathan's parents were out of town and I was home alone waiting for Nathan to get home from work. I was so excited to see him when he got home; I was lonely and felt like a fat cow! All I wanted was a big hug from my husband; to sit, snuggle, and talk about the day. Instead, Nathan walked straight passed me and to the refrigerator. *How typical is that?* I couldn't believe my eyes. He pulled out a beer and starting guzzling.

"What are you doing?" I screamed.

"I'm having a beer what does it look like I'm doing!" He screamed back. It caught me so off guard. I've never seen him drink beer or anything else alcoholic before. I tried to inquire as to why he thought he needed a beer. *Not a good move on my part.* Next thing I knew I was being punched right in the middle of my nine-month pregnant belly! Up to that point, the abuse had all been mental and emotional. Now, it was turning physical. He grabbed his beer and went into the other room. I went and lay down on our bed; streaming tears falling down my face. The next morning it was if nothing had happened. Nathan was his happy, chipper self and treated me like his princess. A couple weeks later, we had our healthy little baby girl, Jaylene. We made the transition from his parent's home to his grandparent's home as planned.

It was only a few weeks before we were able to move into our own one bedroom tiny upstairs apartment that was in an old house that had been converted into individual units. The landlord lived on the lower floor and turned the three upstairs bedrooms into apartments. Two were studio apartments and one, the one we rented, had a bedroom.

Nathan started being physically abusive with me again. I tried to be a good wife and mother, but nothing I could say or do kept him from partying. It got to the point where I just couldn't speak to him unless I was spoken to first. If I spoke out of turn, I found myself flying through the air or getting used like a punching bag in a boxing ring.

Chapter 5

Road Trip with a Newborn

I had to get away from all the abuse; things were getting really crazy. My mom's house was out of the question for her own safety. So I decided to take a road trip home to Spokane. I told Nathan I wanted to take the trip to introduce our new baby to my relatives and friends; he agreed to let me go. How would I pull it off? I had no money and my car wasn't in the best condition to be taking such a long trip. In desperation, I drove up to my mother-in-law's home to ask her for the money to make the trip. Up until now, any bruises she saw on my body were explained as my clumsiness; running into door jams. She knew something was wrong when she saw me pulling into her driveway. She met me at my car and asked what was going on. "I have to get out of town. I have to get away for awhile." Looking over my arms and legs she said, "You didn't get these from running into doorways did you." I shook my head no and tears began streaming down my checks. "I was hoping it wasn't hereditary. Nathan's real father used to abuse me too." We embraced in a hug and she gave me all the cash she had available at the time. "Here, all I have is $80.00, but you need to go to Spokane."

After that, I drove over to my sister's house to let her know I was going out of town for a bit. "With your car?" she asked. "Your car won't make that trip, here, take mine." She had just purchased a nice little car that was in great shape. "I can't take your car, what will you drive?" I asked. "I'll use your car. If it breaks down at least I'll be local and someone can come get me" she said. I was overwhelmed with emotion – the love and willingness of my mother-in-law and my sister to help me get out of town was amazing. I was so very thankful.

When Nathan came home from work, I told him that I'd be leaving in the morning for Spokane. Turns out he was only agreeing to let me go because he knew I didn't have any money and that my car would not make the trip. So knowing that I probably would not be able to follow through with my plans, he agreed to the trip. He was very surprised when I told him I was going. "How are you able to go? I'm not giving you any money," he assured me. "You don't have to, your mom gave me the money . . . yes your mom. Wasn't that nice of her?" I said with a smirk. "And, my sister is letting me use her car so you won't have to worry about mine breaking down along the way." I added. There really wasn't anything he could do at this point. Everything had been provided for me. Reluctantly, he agreed to let me go and promised me that he would phone me every night to see how things were going. My mom called my brother and sister-in-law and asked if I could stay with them for a few days. They agreed and I was all set to go. *(My brother was my youth pastor prior to moving to Oregon, so I knew for sure I would receive great wisdom and advice from him, after all he was a pastor. I fully expected him to tell me the same thing I'd been hearing from other well-meaning people in the church, and that was to stick it through because marriage was a commitment. But he totally surprised me. It was my first sign of hope that maybe it was possible for me to get out of this situation.)*

I had never driven to Spokane all by myself before, let alone with a newborn baby on board. I was very nervous. My mom wrote out every exit I was to take along the way. I drove slower than the other traffic out of my sheer fear of missing one of those exits. I noticed there was a big semi truck following me. He kept a safe distance and I kept wondering why he didn't pass me. Somehow I felt comfort in it. It was nice to have a travel brigade. Jaylene was a great traveling baby. She slept pretty much the whole way, except when she needed to eat. The time came for her feeding so I pulled off to the shoulder just after taking one of the exits on my route. The semi that had been following me also pulled over, again keeping a safe distance. I wasn't sure if I needed to be concerned or what! Was this man climbing down from his truck a serial killer or a Good Samaritan? Before he got too close to me he yelled out, "Is everything okay?" I felt relieved and assured that he was there to help. "Yes, I'm just getting my baby's bottle out of the diaper bag." I replied. He told me that he felt lead to shadow me, and that he was praying for me. My nervousness was very apparent to him and he wanted to be sure that I was okay. I explained that it was my first solo trip driving to Spokane and that I had a newborn in the car and that made me even more cautious. He said a quick prayer with me and told me he had to take the next turn off. He made sure I was comfortable with my map and assured me I would be just fine. WOW. God gave me my own guardian angel. He tooted his big semi air horn as he turned off and waved goodbye. I felt much better after that encounter and made the rest of the trip with more confidence.

It felt so good to be home in Spokane again. I was excited for my family and friends to meet my baby girl. It just so happened that my brother and his wife were expecting their first baby so they graciously allowed me to use their newly decorated nursery for Jaylene.

The trip was bittersweet. I was there to take refuge from all the abuse I was experiencing at home. But I was also there to celebrate the birth of my daughter. My friends and family did not know the extent of the abuse I was living with. I had a hard time telling anyone about it. So I just went about my days pretending everything was good.

One evening, as I was getting ready for bed, my brother came to say goodnight to me. He opened the bedroom door just as I was putting my night gown on. The gown was just falling past my thighs as the door opened. He saw all the bruises on my legs and arms and charged through the door darting right for me. He lifted my gown up just past my knees and asked, "Did he do this to you?" There was anger in his voice like I had never heard from him before. "Yes." I replied in shame.

"Don't you go back to him; you can't go back to him" he firmly exclaimed.

Wait . . . what? "Don't you go back to him?" At that moment, all my preconceived thoughts about what a "pastor" would say went right out the window. Was this really happening? Could I actually leave? Granted, this pastor was also my brother so I can understand the anger and the advice not to return to this abusive situation. But nonetheless, it was freeing for me to hear those words.

It didn't seem to matter that the situation in and of itself was awkward, thankfully my gown was past any parts I wouldn't want my brother to see as he opened the door! What was awkward, however, is the fact that I had now been found out. No more hiding bruises or pretending that everything was fine. The conversation was brief, and it was very apparent how upset and angry my brother was, and rightfully so. When he left the room, I sat down on the edge of the bed. Everything went into "slow motion" mode as flashes of events ran through my mind. He's right. I can't go back. But now what?

I waited by the phone every evening for Nathan's call. I even tried to call him several times, but he never answered. Finally, one evening my brother with great compassion said, "He's not going to call you so stop waiting for him." OUCH! But oh how very true those words were. I couldn't breathe. Feelings of complete aloneness crawled up my spine as I was coming to terms with the reality of my situation. How did all this happen, and, how did it happen to me? Things like this weren't supposed to happen to me. *Nor should they happen for anyone!*

Why wasn't he calling me and what was he doing? I had to find out. So, I packed up a couple days early and drove back home. When I arrived home, Nathan was not there. For some reason, I was still excited to see him and envisioned hugs and kisses, like the kind in the movies when loved ones had been apart. Doesn't absence make the heart grow fonder? I decided to wait out on the balcony; it was a nice day outside. It wasn't too long before I heard his car pulling up to the house. My heart started racing. Perhaps while I was gone, he realized just how much he loved me and would mend his ways. I ran to the railing so I could see him as he walked up the driveway to the door. I couldn't wait to see his bright smile and those big blue eyes. Instead, I saw another girl in the front seat of his car. *(I say girl rather than woman . . . after all; we were only 19 years old.)* A few seconds later, Nathan drove off as fast as he could. He must have seen my sister's car parked in the parking lot and realized I was home early. I dropped to my knees with total unbelief. What did I just see? What was going on? I had to find out.

"Open the door!" I said as I pounded on my neighbor's door. I was on a mission to find out what went on in my apartment while I was gone. I had two neighbors, a single guy in the studio apartment on our left, and a single gal in the other studio apartment on our right. "Please, open the door; I need to talk with you." I repeated. He reluctantly opened the door and said, "I have nothing to say to you; I don't want to get involved." I ran around the stairway landing to my other neighbor's door. "Open the door; I want to talk with you." I said again. She graciously opened the door and invited me in. "I need to know what went on here while I was gone. Did you see anything at all?" I asked. She sat there gazing at me with this look of pity on her face. She kept silent. "Please, I really need to know. My life is in the balance here." I pleaded. After many pleas and coaxing, she finally began to speak. "He had a different girl up here every night; I'm so sorry." She said. Tears started streaming down my cheeks. I took a deep breath, straightened my posture as a breeze of strength began to fill my soul. "Thank you. That's all I need to know." I said.

I knew what I had to do. It was really time to leave. I left my bags packed and waited on the couch for him to come home. It was only twenty minutes until he returned home. Apparently the girl didn't live too far away for him to go drop her off. At first he tried to act all surprised that I was home early and began to put on the charade that he was happy to see me. He had no idea that I was up on that balcony and that I had seen him with the other girl. I let him gush over me for just a few seconds and then I said, "I was on the balcony when you pulled in. I saw you with the other girl."

He made excuses and denied that anything was going on with her. He said she was just a friend who needed a ride home. "Really; then why did you speed off when you realized I was home? Why not invite your friend in to meet your wife?" I asked. Before he could start with his defense again I added, "I talked with the neighbor. She said you had a different girl up here every night. Is that true?" He didn't answer me. I continued, "I think it's best that I find another place to stay. I can no longer sleep in the same bed with you." He didn't deny anything and he didn't try to stop me from leaving.

Where on earth was I going to go? I called a friend and explained the situation. Her mother invited me and my baby to come stay with them. It was perfect, Nathan would have no idea where I was and would not be able to find me if he came looking for me. My mother's house would be way too obvious and I didn't trust him not to go there even though he had a restraining order to do so. This was perfect.

Now, how would I support myself and my baby? I went and visited my old boss from a job I had while I was in high school and explained the situation to him as well. He had so much compassion for me. There were no job openings at the time, but he created one just so I could come and work to earn a paycheck and support my baby and get out of the abusive situation. My friend and her mom watched my baby during the times I had to work. It truly was amazing how things fell into place.

Nathan never did find out where I was staying. I took every precaution when driving home to make sure he was nowhere around to follow me. He did find out that I was working at my old job again though and there were a few times he came looking for me while I was at work. Every employee in the store knew the situation and had a photo of Nathan so they could protect me in the event he came looking for me. We even had to call the police at one time to come and remove him from the property of the store. These people were amazing to put up with such drama. God really had orchestrated all of this and kept me safe.

My friend and her mom were also truly gracious and such a blessing to me. But I knew I couldn't stay there forever. I had saved enough money for me to begin thinking about getting my own apartment. My mom and I began looking in Salem, OR. There was no point for me to stay in Silverton any longer. Besides, it would be nice to be back closer to my mom and other family and friends. We found the perfect little two-bedroom apartment. My mom put the deposit down for me so I could use my money for the rent and a few essentials I would need to help furnish the place. I was truly grateful.

A few weeks later, somehow, someway, Nathan managed to turn on his charm and with apology after apology managed to work his way back into my heart and into my new apartment. He finished his internship at the Nursing Home and dropped out of school. He was offered a job at the Nursing Home, but he no longer was interested in that line of work. So, he got a job at a woodworking place back in Silverton. The shop was owned by his best friend's parents; who were partiers themselves and included Nathan in all their parties. The abuse continued, but at a higher level of intensity. Nathan was drinking, doing drugs, partying, and sleeping around with other girls.

Chapter 6

The Rent Race

I found myself again at the point where I couldn't take any more abuse from him. I asked him to move out. But he refused. We argued day after day about who had to move out and who got to have the apartment. The fact that my mom paid all the deposits and the apartment was originally intended just for Jaylene and I meant nothing to him. Knowing that I didn't have a good steady income as a Tupperware dealer, he threw out this challenge, "Here is how we will decide this." He said with a smirk. "The rent is due in two weeks. Whoever can pay the rent in full first gets the apartment."

I knew he had a payday in one week and that I didn't have a chance in Vegas of winning this one, but I yelled back at him, "Agreed. Two weeks and you're out of here!"

Oh lord, I thought to myself, how in the world am I going to pay the rent by myself? Rent was $400.00. After Nathan left for work, my brain went into overdrive thinking of how I was going to do this! I had to get $400.00 before Nathan's payday. My friend Maria came to mind. I knew she was attending a Bible College just a few blocks down from my apartment. How cool would it be if she could be my roommate and live closer to school? I called her up, asked if she was interested in being my roommate, and explained the situation to her. She agreed! I couldn't believe it! She brought me her share of the rent, $200.00, within a couple days. I had no idea how I would get my share of the rent. I didn't want to ask my mom for the money. She was already pretty upset that Nathan moved back in with us in the first place. That same week, I had a letter arrive from Eugene Bible College. Enclosed was a check for $200.00. I about dropped to the floor. Again, my water works started up and tears overwhelmed my eyes and made their long trek down my face.

The letter stated this:

> Enclosed is your Kiwanis Scholarship money that was awarded to you in 1982. Scholarships are not usually redeemed until the 2nd semester, but since you left during the first semester the check was never applied. We found the money when we were going through our records. Normally, we send the check back to the grantor but for some reason, we felt lead to forward the check to you. Hope you are doing well.

It had been one full year since I left the college. It was if the sky opened up and all the heavens were singing, and sunbeams were streaming down on me. It was a glorious moment. I ran down to the manager's office and signed the check over to her. I didn't even cash it, just signed it over. The rent was paid! The relief of all relief poured over my heart. I called Maria and she started moving in that day!

I put Nathan's suitcase on the bed. When he got home that evening, I told him he lost the challenge, the rent was paid. Thankfully Maria was there, it probably saved me from another beating. Maria and I both stood together and made sure he knew he was the one moving out - not me! He had nowhere to go and asked for a few days to find a place. We agreed. A few days turned into a few weeks. Finally, the day came when Nathan moved out. It was just Jaylene, Maria, and me! We turned the apartment into a sweet little home and I finally felt safe again. I had resolved that divorce was going to be the route I'd have to take. This went against every fiber in my being, again because of my Christian upbringing, but I knew it was the only way. I told Nathan that I would be filing for divorce as soon as I could afford to. I kept stalling though. Somehow I kept thinking either he is going to die of an overdose or car accident from being drunk and stoned all the time, or God will do something miraculous and Nathan would stop beating me and give his life back to God.

Chapter 7

Doug Who?

Having Maria as a roommate was a blessing. She brought so much life to the place and she would bring her friends form Bible College over to hang out. I was meeting new people and having fun. One day, Maria looked at me and said, "I think you need to meet Doug."

"WHAT?" I exclaimed. "No way, I'm not meeting anybody."

"But you two have a lot in common; I think you would have a lot to talk about." She explained.

"NO! I don't want to meet him." I reiterated again. At that moment, I heard a whisper in my ear. *That's who I have for you.* I turned around to see who was whispering in my ear, but nobody was there.

A few days later, Maria started in again. "I really think you need to meet Doug." Shaking my head side-to-side I said, "No way, the last thing I want to do is meet a guy." Once more I heard: *That's who I have for you.*

I looked around again, and there was nobody there to whisper in my ear. "Okay Maria, if this Doug guy is so great, why aren't you dating him? What's wrong with him?" I asked.

"EWWWW, that would be like dating my brother," she said. "We are really good friends, I don't think of him in that way." Then I really wondered what was wrong with him. I stood strong and insisted she not bring him home to meet me.

Later that week, Jaylene was having a horrible night sleeping. She was teething and didn't feel well. She cried and screamed most of the night until around 4 A.M. When it was finally quiet, and I could get a few Z's in myself before her next feeding, I had a hard time falling back to sleep.

Get up, Maria's bringing Doug home. The Holy Spirit, with those words, awakened me. "What? Not today God, I had a horrible night's sleep." I groaned. *Get up, Maria's bringing Doug home.* The Holy Spirit said again.

It was 10 A.M. in the morning. I had about five hours of sleep by then. "Fine, I'll get up!" I grumbled. I fumbled my way into the bathroom and took a shower. All my clothes were dirty and in the laundry basket. I thought to myself, "Well, if Maria is going to bring Doug home to meet me I'm borrowing her jeans!" So, I went into her closet and picked out a great pair of jeans and a very cute shirt to wear. I figured it was the least she could do for me since she was the one bringing home the guy I didn't even want to meet. I then got the brainy idea to make lunch for them when everyone arrived. School was out at noon and I knew it wouldn't be long until a bunch of college mates walked through the door.

My options for lunch were hot dogs or . . . hot dogs. I went with the hot dogs! I was ready to meet Doug. I looked good in Maria's clothes, and the hot dogs were boiled and ready to eat.

Surely hot dogs would win the heart of any man. I don't know why I was even stressing – I didn't even want to meet him! Sure enough, at about five minutes after noon, a strange tan car pulled up and parked in front of the kitchen window. Maria got out of the passenger's side and began to walk towards the front door. I glanced over to the driver's side and caught a glimpse of Doug through the windshield of his car. *That's all it took. I was smitten.*

"Wow, he's really good looking!" I said out loud in a room all alone. I gave my hair one last toss over and poised myself in front of the stove. The door opened and Maria and Doug walked through.

"Jan, this is Doug, Doug, this is Jan." Maria spouted. Our eyes connected and we both smiled. It was an instant connection.

"Would you like some lunch? I made hot dogs." Those were the first words out of my mouth. Not "Hi," not "Nice to meet you," but "Would you like some lunch, I made hot dogs."

But to my surprise he kindly replied; "Yes, that would be great."

And so our journey began . . . over a hot dog. We sat on the couch eating our hot dogs talking and laughing. A few minutes later Maria announced it was time for Doug's haircut. Another college friend was there with us apparently to cut Doug's hair.

At 10 A.M., the same time God was waking me up, Doug was asking the girls to give him a haircut after school. They usually did the haircuts on campus but this time, Maria decided to have them come to the apartment. Doug didn't even know I existed. All he knew was that he was going to Maria's for a haircut. All the while Maria was talking to me about Doug; she didn't mention me to him, not even once. I was a complete surprise to him. But apparently, he liked his surprise. Like I said, it was an instant connection and we hit it off. October 6, 1983 at 12:05 P.M. his life would never be the same…and neither would mine.

The next day Doug dropped by my apartment with a box full of used baby clothes. He brought them over for Jaylene. If I hadn't fallen for him the day before, this surely would have done the trick! We saw each other every afternoon between his college classes and him going to work. We had three hours every afternoon that we spent together with some of Maria and Doug's other college friends. Our apartment was now "The hang out place." And I loved it! I felt like my life was gaining some sort of normalcy again and I had the support of great friends who encouraged me and helped me with my baby. We were a family of college groupies!

Chapter 8

God Sent Me a Guardian Angel

One day after lunch the college group dispersed and went their separate ways; I was home all-alone with Jaylene. A couple hours later, there was a knock at the door. It was Doug. He had just left for work not too long ago, so I wondered what could possibly bring him by now. I opened the door and asked what he was doing here.

He looked very surreal and said, "I don't know. I was working laying carpet when I heard the Holy Spirit telling me to get back over here." I let him in and we sat at the kitchen table. Jaylene was napping so it was very quiet.

"I don't know why I'm here I just know I'm supposed to be here." Doug reiterated.

"Okay, then we'll just wait," I said. He began to work on some homework and we chit-chatted here and there as I went about my routine of cleaning the apartment. Not too long after Doug arrived, there was a knock at the door. It was Nathan. I knew it was him because he drove a very loud Volkswagen square-back and I heard him pull into the parking lot. I answered the door and asked him what he wanted.

"Can I come in?" He asked.

"Sure, come on in," I responded. As he walked around the corner, he spotted Doug sitting at the table. It seemed to have jilted him a bit to see someone else in the apartment. He figured I'd be alone. When we explained he was a friend of Maria's and he was working on homework, he seemed to relax a bit. He then asked me if he could hold Jaylene. That really threw me for a loop because for the past 3 months he refused to hold her or even look at her.

"Yes!" I exclaimed with a hopeful voice. "She's asleep but I'll wake her up." I was just thrilled that he wanted to hold his baby. I brought Jaylene out and handed her to Nathan. He sat down on the couch with her and just held her and talked to her. It was so precious to watch. My heart filled with hope and my eyes filled with tears. He handed her back to me and I put her back in her crib. He then gave me a children's Bible. It was his from when he was a little boy. He asked me to make sure Jaylene would get it one day.

I handed it back and said, "You give it to her someday that would be more appropriate."

He handed it back and said. "Please just promise me she will have this one day." I felt a sense of gloom in the air, took the Bible back, and assured him I would give her the Bible when she was old enough to have it.

He then looked at my telephone. "Can I use your phone?" He asked.

"Of course you can," I answered.

"Okay, but understand, I'm making a long distance call and I won't be able to repay you for the charges." He explained.

"Who are you calling?" I asked.

"I'm calling my parents." With a huge lump in my throat, I nodded and gave him permission to use the phone. Again, it had been over three months without him speaking to his parents, either. My mind was racing. What was going on? Why is he making amends with everyone all of a sudden? Just a few days prior to that he had made amends with my mom. They had a long walk and they prayed together. He even threw away all his drugs. I had agreed to wait for him, but only if he would go to counseling. I told him he was not moving back into the apartment until he got the help he needed, and I was sure he was changing for the right reasons. He had agreed. *So, was he really going to follow through with this change after all?*

He called his parents. Hearing one-sided conversations are always interesting, but this one was a bit eerie. He said things like; *I love you, no I don't want anything from you, I just called to tell you I love you, no I'm not asking for money.* And then he said, "She's here sitting with her boyfriend. No, I don't blame her."

After he hung up the phone, he stood at the hallway and poised himself to look straight into Doug's eyes. He said. "Dude, you just better take care of her a lot better than I did." He then straightened his stance, raised his right hand, formed his arm into a saluting position, and began to hum the tune to "Taps." When he was finished, he walked out the door.

"That was so weird," I said.

Doug agreed and stated that he felt he needed to stick around a little longer. I said, "Okay" and Doug went back to doing homework. Over the next couple of hours, I could hear Nathan calling my name from outside. I knew from previous patterns that if I opened the door this time around, it would be my turn to get hurt. One visit was an apology; the next was a beating. I grew accustomed to this cycle.

A couple hours later my mom called to let me know my Aunt and Uncle had come to town to visit and that they wanted to see me and meet Jaylene. We arranged to meet at the nearby Dairy Queen. I asked if I could bring Doug along and she said, "Absolutely!" By this time, mom and Doug had a great relationship, too. Doug got Jaylene in the car seat and carried her out to the car for me.

"Where are you going?" Nathan shouted from some unknown location. I looked around and couldn't see him anywhere.

"Where are you? We're going to meet my mom at Dairy Queen. My Aunt and Uncle are there too - the ones you like. Why don't you come with us?" I offered. But he didn't reply.

We waited a bit and then I turned to Doug and said, "Forget it, let's just go." The very moment I turned back around to face the car, the field on the other side of the fence that separated the parking lot from the church property next door went up in a blaze of fire.

I couldn't believe it. Now Nathan is doing arson?

"Doug, he just set that field on fire! Why would he do that?" I asked.

"Um, I don't think he set the field on fire, I think he set himself on fire." Doug responded.

"No way, he wouldn't do that, he's just doing arson." I proclaimed.

"Janice, go in the house and dial 9-1-1, NOW." Doug demanded.

Thank goodness Doug was holding Jaylene! I'm not sure what I would have done. Doug took me by the arm and escorted me back inside the apartment. I still didn't see what the big deal was. Sure, I needed to call the fire department because Nathan set the field on fire, but I didn't believe that Nathan could be *in* the fire. Doug picked up the phone and dialed 9-1-1, and then handed me the phone. He still had Jaylene in his arms.

"9-1-1 what is your emergency please?"

I answered, "There's a field on fire next door to my apartment, and I think there may be someone in it." The operator kept me on the phone for a few minutes while they found the location and had the fire trucks deployed and on their way to the scene.

By the time we got back outside, there were people gathered along the fence line watching the event take place. The fire truck was already there and working on putting out the fire. Still not believing that Nathan was in the fire I began to look really hard at the fire to see if I could see anything. I spotted what looked like an arm sticking up in the air and I calmly asked Doug, "Is that an arm?" Pointing to what I was seeing.

"Yes, I think so," he replied. It was the strangest thing, I felt so calm and at peace. I knew somehow I would never be hurt again by Nathan's abuse if he was indeed in the fire. The next thought I had was that I ought to help the firefighters know that if there was a body in the fire, I could at least tell them who it was. I asked Doug to come with me and we walked the fence line down to the street and back up the other side to where the fire truck was parked. The fire chief met us and started to tell us we couldn't be there and asked us to leave.

"Was there a body in that fire?" I asked.

The fire chief stopped and said, "Yes there was."

"Then I know who it was." I explained. I went on to say, "It was my husband." At that moment, the fire chief tore his jacket off and threw it over my head as he grabbed me and turned me around. He yelled, "GET HER OUT OF HERE!"

At that point my commonsense told me that "Oh, I'm not supposed to be calm, I'm supposed to be hysterical." All calmness left me as I began to scream. The fire chief and Doug escorted me back to my apartment.

The very moment the field went up in flames; my roommate and her friend were turning into the parking lot to come home. They were at a wedding reception and she too heard the Holy Spirit telling her to get back home; just as he had told Doug to get over to my place earlier that day.

Maria came running up to me and said, "Nathan was in there wasn't he?"

I nodded yes and she embraced me in her arms. I suddenly remembered that we were on our way to see my family. I asked Maria and her friend to please drive to the Dairy Queen and get my mom. *(We didn't have cell phones then.)* By the time they returned, my apartment was filled with police officers, the fire chief, the pastor of the church next door and some friends. It was a full house. Our youth pastor showed up shortly thereafter. Ironically, the pastor of the church next door was the pastor that married Nathan and I. He had moved church locations. He was a friend of the family. I felt badly that this all took place behind his church. After speaking with the police and fire chiefs, and answering all their questions, the fire chief squatted down to my eye level and said, "It was a good thing you were not home alone. If you had been, he would have had no hesitation to set this apartment on fire taking you and the baby with him." *Wow*!

Shortly after things started to quiet down, it hit me. I have to call Nathan's parents! Nathan just called them earlier that day to tell them he loved them. They are going to be crushed. I picked up the phone and dialed the number. As I explain what happened, my mother-in-law did not believe me. She insisted on talking to someone else. I handed the phone to someone, I honestly cannot remember to whom, and they went on to explain that I was telling the truth. Their son was dead. They drove to Salem from Silverton immediately after the phone call ended. When they arrived, my mother-in-law embraced me and whispered, "I do not want you to blame yourself for this. This was not your fault."

I asked her to explain what she meant. She said, "Nathan had a pattern his whole life. He was either a Christian, or a total backslider. He had no in between. He changed every two years or so, either being very good, or being very bad.

"Why didn't you tell me before?" I asked.

She said, "Because when he was with you he was at his best most of the time and we had hoped that you would be the one to keep him on the good side." She then offered to take care of all the funeral arrangements and expenses. She said it was her responsibility and she wanted to do it. Her only stipulation was Nathan had to be interred at the family church and the memorial had to be Episcopalian. With a huge sigh of relief, I agreed. *After all; how in the world would I be able to afford all that?*

"He was your son longer than he was my husband, if that's what you want, then that's what I want." I said. We hugged and moved on into the living room where the rest of the crowd had gathered.

It suddenly hit me that I had no clue where my baby was! In a moment of brief panic I started to yell, "Where's my baby?"

The crowd parted just like the Red Sea did and at the other end of the room was someone holding my baby. She was sound asleep. We walked towards each other through the parted crowd of people and she handed me my baby. I sat down on the couch with that four-month-old baby girl, I held her close to my chest, and I began to weep. The room was silent. I rocked my baby in my arms and I said, "It's just me and you now baby, but we're safe and I'm going to take care of you always."

For the next several nights, the college groupies all camped out in our apartment with us. They kept me on a 24-hour watch schedule. I wasn't to be left alone. It was the most loving and sacrificial thing I had experienced in a long time. I felt very blessed.

Commonsense would tell me that I needed to move out of the apartment; that I wouldn't be able to live next to the scene of the crime. I went down to the manager's office to turn in my 30-day notice. The manager asked me to sit down.

"How are you doing?" She asked.

"I'm doing pretty well all things considered," I replied.

"Why do you want to move, are you having nightmares?" She inquired.

"No, just seems the thing to do. Oddly enough, I'm not having any nightmares. In fact, I feel a sense of relief that I'm safe now," I answered.

"Well, it's too bad you want to move, because this complex just turned into a low income property and your rent is being lowered to $165.00 a month." She explained. "Still feel like moving?" She asked.

"Nope, I think I'll be staying right where I am," I smiled.

She said, "Good, because I like you." We hugged and I went to share the news with my roommate that she would not have to move after all.

I finally had my first breakdown a few days after Nathan died. The college groupies were still staying at the apartment and I just broke down in a terrified manner. "I killed him! I killed him! He used the money he got from me to buy the gas with! He told me he needed gas money to get to work. I wasn't going to give it to him, but he threatened to beat me up; I had no choice. He used that money to buy the gasoline that he used on himself!" I was horrified. My friends embraced me and assured me that it was not my fault, that he would have found the money somewhere else anyway, and that Nathan was responsible for killing himself.

The memorial service was beautiful. There were so many people there to show their love and support to the family. I didn't know half of them; they were there for Nathan's family. A lot of my friends and family were also there. I truly felt loved.

This all took place late in October, one month shy of our one-year anniversary, which was to be in November. Nathan's death hit me hard. I had such a loving and perfect life growing up; I had no idea that this kind of pain existed. I didn't know what to do or where to turn. I tried to push through and live as normally as I could. But I was walking around in a great state of shock.

So, there I was, single again. I began to get phone calls from many of my ex-boyfriends. All of them wanting to make sure I was okay and offering to help in any way they could. I even got asked out on some dates. While I was very flattered, the last thing I wanted to do was date. I graciously thanked them for calling and assured them I would be all right. Doug and I grew closer, but we never did officially "date." We just always hung out and talked.

Thanksgiving time came around and my mom and I planned a trip to Spokane to see family and friends for the holiday. I was excited! It surprised me that I started missing Doug while we were away. I had no business even thinking about entering into a relationship at that time. I was a mess! We talked on the phone every day that I was gone. He made me laugh, smile, and for whatever reason I couldn't explain, we had a strong connection.

When I returned home to Oregon, Doug was there to meet me with open arms and a surprise: A dozen red long stemmed roses and a promise ring right in the middle of one of the blossoms. I knew Doug was the one I was supposed to be with. The words, "That's who I have for you" kept coming to my mind. I knew I had to trust that it was God giving me my knight in shining armor.

Over the next few weeks, I started feeling extreme pain within my body. I had been kicked around, boxed around, and thrown around for the past five months. My back was out of alignment from when Nathan ran full speed across an open field and karate kicked me right in the middle of my chest. That kick had knocked me backwards several feet and I landed squarely on my back. I was also experiencing very painful cramping and very sore ovaries. I decided I needed to get some medical attention. So I made appointments for the chiropractor and for the Doctor.

My first stop was the chiropractor. My back was pretty messed up from all the abuse. I was looking forward to the series of adjustments I would be receiving to help relieve the pain and get my spine back into alignment.

Next, I went to the doctor's office for a complete physical. After a long examination and some tests, the doctor came back into the room and announced that I was pregnant. I couldn't believe it! Nathan and I had sex not to long before his death. *I guess I was still attempting to save the marriage and oftentimes would give into his charming ways.* The doctor asked me what I wanted to do.

I was nineteen years old. I was in shock and I had no clue what was happening. I was in no place to know what was right or what was wrong. The doctor said we only had a short window of time and I needed to make my decision as soon as possible. His strong recommendation, based on the recent events, Nathan's drug and alcohol usage, and my overall mental well being was for me to abort the baby.

The next week I went in to the doctor's office and had an abortion. It was probably the shortest procedure I've ever had done. When the doctor was through, he patted me on the shoulder and said, "It's done, you made the right decision."

Did I? Did I make the right decision? What I did went against my beliefs. I was mortified and distraught. Ashamed and feeling guilty.

Chapter 9

I Do

Doug and I were married on January 6, 1984, exactly three months to the day that we met. It was a beautiful wedding, and well attended. We had the support and love of many of our friends and family, even though we had only known each other for three short months and that it was a bit too soon after Nathan's death to be getting remarried. But we just knew it was right. Jaylene was seven months old by then. Doug took her in as his own daughter and raised her with no inhibitions.

At first, everything seemed to be going great. Doug was in his third year of Bible College and he was going to be a pastor. My dream from girlhood was coming true. I was going to be a pastor's wife after all! But then the shock factor of all the events that had previously happened started wearing off. I began to emerge from this place of darkness and realized that I was living a whole new life and I had no idea how I had gotten here.

I woke up one morning at about 7 A.M. - the time I was supposed to be in jazz choir class when I was in high school. "Oh man, Cooper is going to kill me if I'm late for class one more time!" I bounced out of bed and began to get ready for school. I heard a baby crying in the other room. "Wait, why is there a baby crying? Whose baby is that? Oh wait, I think it's mine! I have a baby. I'm married. Who am I married to? Nathan, no wait,

Doug." It was all in a moment's instant that all these things ran through my mind, but it seemed like an eternity. Things were playing in slow motion and my thinking voice was very loud in my head. "I'm married to Doug, I have a daughter, and I'm not in high school anymore." I couldn't remember my wedding to Doug. *Yep, the shock factor had finally worn off!* It didn't take too long before details of my wedding returned. In reality, it was probably all in a split second. It was one of the strangest mental moments I've ever experienced.

Anger began to set-in to replace the shock. When Doug returned home from work that evening, I made it very clear that I had no business being married to him! I didn't know who I was, or what I was doing. But I had no place being remarried to someone I didn't even know! I tried everything in my power to make this man want to leave me. I tried to push him to levels of anger so he'd hit me. Then I'd have a real excuse for leaving him! I told him I didn't love him. I told him I didn't want to be married to him.

But he was patient...

He never hit me, and he never fought back. He only looked me in the eyes and said, "I love you and I'm here for you." This struggle went on for weeks. I even went as far as pretending to have a date with a co-worker. I told him I was going out to dinner with a man from work and I was in love with him. Doug opened the front door for me and said these words. "Have a great time on your date. But remember, you are married to me so you can't touch him."

I heard this small still voice in my head, *don't blow this. He is the real deal.* I shut the door and took off my coat. *I didn't even have a date, anyways.* But hearing those words, and seeing his love for me made me realize that Doug was my gift from God, and even though we probably got married too soon, he was the one God had intended for me.

From anger, I went to having denial and nightmares. I had this overwhelming sense that Nathan was not dead. I could almost *feel* his presence. There were times I thought I saw him in crowds when we were at the mall or at a park. My dreams became horrifying. Nathan was coming after me to take me with him. I couldn't close my eyes at night. I was exhausted and worn out from Nathan's haunting.

Once the anger and nightmare stage passed, I fell into a deep depression. At first, I was able to function pretty well, but over the years, I became increasingly manically depressed. In 1985, Doug and I had our son. When Jeremy joined our little family, we were thrilled, but I was still depressed.

Chapter 10

Full Circle

In 1989, Doug and I returned to Eugene Bible College so he could convert his diploma into a degree and I could finish my education at the ripe old age of twenty-five. I was once again singing in one of the college groups, traveling and ministering to youth all over the Northwest. *There were many moments where I felt God restoring my hopes and dreams. Returning to Eugene Bible College was very instrumental in my healing. My life was rewound to the very spot it fell apart. I had a second chance at my dreams.*

I spent the next ten years in a state of depression, but pretending to be okay, functioning as a "whole person" – at least to the outside world, I was. Doug and I held positions in ministry as youth pastors and associate pastors. Doug had a great job in the auto parts and service industry. We had two great kids and lots of friends. From the outside, we seemed to be perfectly normal. But there came a point when I just couldn't do it on my own any longer. Again, because of my Christian upbringing, I felt I couldn't seek professional help or take any antidepressant drugs. That was a big taboo at that time within the church. But, I finally had no other option. I agreed to seek professional help. Ten years after the traumatic events, I was diagnosed with Post Traumatic Stress Disorder and was prescribed an antidepressant.

At the time, we were in the middle of starting a new church in Salem, OR. Doug and I felt very strongly that it was time to step-down from ministry and focus on getting me well. We called our superintendants and invited them to come by the house so we could talk. As we shared our journey and the recent diagnosis I received, it was very clear to us that they did not approve. They told me not to take the antidepressant because I would become addicted to it. We resigned our position and that was that. There was no real empathy or compassion from this arena. We felt rejected and alone. We felt judged.

God is a redeeming God. And through my journey from trauma to joy, there are countless moments of God's divine healing. Everything I lost, He has returned to me in full. Every dream I dreamt He has painted in living color. Every breath I take is because of His hand of protection on my life. Yes, we serve a redeeming God. And He can redeem you too. My story is like so many of your stories. We all have a journey. Some full of heartbreak and tragedy, but in the midst of our sorrow and mourning, God is there with His arms open wide waiting for you and I to embrace Him and to allow Him to make us whole again. There is purpose. There is Joy. There is Hope - even after the traumatic events in our lives have left our hearts in pieces. As you continue to read Part Two of this book, I pray that you will be able to work through whatever areas that have been holding you back from living a whole and fulfilled life in Christ; for redemption is for all of us.

Section Two
Scenes that Played Out

Chapter 11

Another confirmation please; I didn't like the first one!

Have you ever asked God to give you confirmation about something, and then when you received it, you asked for another confirmation to confirm the first confirmation? Why do we do that? I wonder what God thinks when we do that. Many of us know how exasperating it is to have someone ask us for the same thing over and over and over. However, in this particular case, I'm thankful that God didn't grow weary of my pleas, even though I just wanted to make sure that I knew that I knew that I knew! The funny thing is, even after receiving two confirmations from God, I still ignored them and did nothing. Okay, well that's not so funny – but it all worked out in the end!

By being born and raised in the pew, so to speak, I had very strong convictions poured into me my whole life. My cup was full and running over with the Kool-Aid of religion. I had it down pat! And, like many of you, divorce was not a word I had in my vocabulary. So even though I was being horribly abused physically, verbally, and mentally by my husband, I stood tall and proclaimed, "Divorce is NOT an option!" Besides, I assumed as we so wrongly do, that God would change my husband. *Have you ever tried to change someone who doesn't want to be changed?*

Hiding my bruises while singing in the choir

Often I would cry out to God asking him if it was okay to leave. But, since I had already assumed God would say no, I never took the time to listen for His answer—until this one day.

Between the mattress and box-spring is no place for a knife!

I was home with my newborn baby just cleaning, cooking, and thinking. And as I was sitting on my bed feeding her, I kept wondering and praying. Somehow, in the midst of my thoughts, Jaylene decided to fling her bottle and it rolled across the other side of the bed and onto the floor. Now, I know that it's not *too* unusual to have flying objects suddenly materialize when with a baby, but in this case, it really was a long stretch…the bottle could have just stopped on the bed. But no, this bottle fell down to the floor, which caused me to have to retrieve it. As I laid her on the bed, so I could roll over and reach down again, I prayed, "Please Lord, show me that it's okay to leave."

As I reached my hand down to pick up the bottle I looked over the edge of the bed, I found way more than I bargained for! There, sticking-out from between the mattress and the box-spring, was the handle of a huge hunting knife. YES – a knife hiding in the middle of my bed! I was horrified just thinking about how easy it would have been for him to inconspicuously reach down and pull out that knife. Just one wrong word is all it would have taken to do just that. Recent history with us thus far had already shown me that if I started a conversation at the wrong moment, or by bringing up a topic he did not want to discuss, I ended up as his personal football. I learned very quickly to keep my mouth shout and to wait until I was spoken to first.

I also knew that if I removed the knife completely from the room, I'd be in big trouble, so I pulled the knife out from its hiding place and pushed it under the bed. Afterwards, I retrieved the bottle and continued with Jaylene's feeding.

As I sat there, I pleaded with God again. I prayed, "God, please! I need to know if it's okay to leave. Please!" All of a sudden, a Scripture reference popped into my head. I chuckled a bit and imagined how wonderful it would be if the verse in question just said, "Go." However, since my Bible was not nearby at the time, I put the verse to the back of my mind to look up at a later moment.

Further on in the evening, as I was cooking dinner, the same Scripture reference popped back into my head. I shouted to myself, "Oh yeah, I was supposed to look that up!" I ran into the living room where my Bible was and quickly turned the pages hoping to find my answer!

"Go your way, I am sending you out as a lamb among the wolves." (Luke 10:3) Now, I don't know about you, but I had a hard time believing that was really the verse God was trying to give me! I slammed my Bible shut tight and said "No way, no way!" I decided instantly that I must have surely known that this verse was there. I must have planted that reference in my head not GOD! Although, in all honesty, I never recalled reading that verse before – I'm sure I've heard it at some point in my life prior to this event – but I truly *read* those words for the first time that evening.

Hiding my bruises while singing in the choir

Another confirmation, please!

I needed to be sure I was hearing God correctly, I put a little extra padding in my prayer and prayed; "God, if this is you and you're saying I can really go…I'm going to need another confirmation, please!" I needed to know that it wasn't my own recollection of a Scripture. I needed to know that it wasn't me hearing only what I wanted to hear.

Later on that evening, after Nathan had gotten home and we were getting ready for bed, I was lying there just hoping he wouldn't notice that the knife was gone. Sure enough, as soon as I finished the thought, he asked the dreaded question, "Where's my knife; I had a knife here!"

Within a split second, as I scrambled for my words, I suddenly blurted out "Yeah, I almost cut myself on it while I was making the bed this morning. It's under the bed; I forgot to put it back. I'm sorry."

I prayed, "Thank you Jesus for that cover up," but, of course, I felt horrible for lying. *After all, I was a Christian, and Christians don't lie.* However, Nathan volunteered that the horrid knife was there for protection from would-be robbers. *That was comforting to know, I suppose.* Nevertheless, I proceeded to ask him why he thought we would get robbed.

Nathan replied, "I don't trust my drug buddies. They're dangerous and I fear they might come and try to hurt you or the baby. I need to be ready for them in order to protect you." *Hmmmm...now that's something I wanted to hear before bedtime!* Still, I was very fortunate that night because I completely felt God's hand of protection on my life.

The following morning, just after Nathan left for work, and I was still lying in bed, there was a knock on my door.

"Who knocks on my door at 7:30 in the morning?" I grumbled. I couldn't imagine who it could be. Anyway, I pulled myself out of bed and very cautiously asked who was there; all the while praying it wasn't one of those "drug buddies." *That would be bad – but at least I knew where the knife was hidden (wink-wink)!*

But, to my surprise, it was my mother. She lived thirty minutes away in the next town over. I asked myself, "What was my mother doing at my door at 7:30 A.M., and why?" Her voice sounded urgent, very much like Angela Lansbury from the TV show "Murder She Wrote." My mother had been sitting down the street in her car, watching for Nathan to leave, so she could come by and talk to me.

Her rampant response was, "The Lord woke me up in the middle of the night and told me that you have to get out of here – you're in danger!"

I thought to myself, "Well, good morning to you too!" Nevertheless, even though I felt horrible that she was up all night worrying about me, I was thoroughly amazed at her words. God was showing up again to tell me it was okay to leave. So, how's that for a second confirmation?

As is typical for me, I didn't get the hint. I don't know why I didn't just pack up everything right there and leave with her. Well, I suppose one reason could have been the fact that my husband had already thrown one dining room chair at her a couple of months prior to this. Therefore, protecting my mother from Nathan was very high on my priority list, which is why she had waited down the street for him to leave. We both knew her house would be the first place he would look for me if I had left. That being the case, I told my mom I would find a safe place to go, if going was to be my path, and that I would keep her posted.

It took me a couple more days, but I eventually ended up retreating to a friend's home; and I was safe. Safe! Unfortunately, over the course of several weeks, I moved out and then back home again a grand total of ten times! I just couldn't shake what was ingrained in me from the time I was a small child. Divorce was not an option for Christians. I felt so guilty each time I moved out that I moved right back in! Needless to say - the abuse got worse every time I went back.

However I share this particular part of my story with you because, looking back on it now, I've become so amazed by God's faithfulness! Even through these horrible circumstances, His hand was on me and he was speaking to me. Many times, I didn't take the time to hear Him because I had my own pre-formed ideas of what He would say; nevertheless, He was and is, there.

❧Making Application in Your Life☙

Do you find yourself seeking confirmations to things in your life? If so, I urge you not to discount the little things that might be pointing you in the right direction. We often want some dramatic sign we'll be sure not to miss! Just like a scene in a movie, we beg God for a sign. Do you remember the moment in the 2003 film, Bruce Almighty, *where Bruce's character is praying, "God just show me a sign..." while he's driving behind a huge truck carrying lots of road signs? He had every sign imaginable staring him in the face! But he failed to read any of them. If you are seeking answers for something in your life right now, take the time to really listen for God to speak to you. God speaks in so many ways. You will be amazed at how He will speak to you. The important thing is that you're open to hear his voice and then act upon what He is saying.*

I'm thankful everyday that God didn't grow weary of my pleading for confirmation upon confirmation! Now when I feel that tug, or get an overwhelming feeling to do something, I gladly do it! And, I say, "Thank you God for your direction in my life!"

Chapter 12

Choir Robes Don't Hide Black Eyes

Music has always been a big part of my life. In many ways, music has been my lifeline in so many situations. No matter how many bruises I had, or how mentally torn down I was, singing always provided me an outlet from the reality of my pain. To this day, singing, leading worship, or just listening to music is a source of inspiration and healing for me. I'm not sure what I would have done had I not had music as my outlet. At the same time, I used it as a way of hiding my world. As long as all my bruises were hidden under that choir robe, I felt "normal." I was one of the main soloists in the choir at a fairly large church. In those early years with Nathan, choir practice was every Wednesday night and the choir sang every Sunday. No matter what problems I was facing, every Wednesday I would put my baby in the nursery and attend practice as if nothing was wrong. Every Sunday, I'd do the same thing. But in reality, I was a mess...

Anyone can figure out how to hide bruises. But, depending on where the bruises were, would determine if I would "make it" to choir that day. Most of the time, my bruises were on my upper arms and on my legs. These types of bruises make slacks or long skirts and quarter length sleeves on shirts the perfect match. The fact that my choir really did wear choir robes helped a lot, as well.

Often I would wear a light sweater over a short sleeved or sleeveless dress during the summertime. It was easy to slip the choir robe on and then remove the sweater so I wouldn't get too hot on the platform. A couple of times I did have to "call in sick;" no amount of clothing, including the choir robe, could cover me when I had black eyes.

Even though it wasn't very often that I had physical bruises on my face or any type of a black eye, the few times my face was actually involved, boy were they doozies! One time I sported two black eyes at the same time. That was definitely a weekend I "called in sick" for choir. There was no hiding those shiners underneath a choir robe.

Sometimes the brawls were short and to the point while others were long and intense. And trust me – I fought back with every ounce of my 105 pound body! I'm pretty sure my long nails tore up a lot of skin during those breakout sessions. I'm not one to roll over and play dead very often. And during the time of the two black eyes, there was a definite need for me to fight back...

As with most abusers, it was in my refusal to give Nathan what he wanted that the violence would become more dangerous. In this case, he was after money. Usually by pushing back on him a bit I could stop any further hitting once it had begun. But this time he must have really needed the money for something because he was not about to go anywhere until I gave him what he came for. Unfortunately, I had no money that time around. So, as punishment, he left me with two black eyes, and lots of bumps and bruises. This was one of the few times he actually picked me up and threw me against the wall. And I, in my infinite wisdom of the time, thought to myself; "I live in an apartment. I have two neighbors, one upstairs and one on the other side of this wall I keep getting thrown up against, so they must be hearing this?" That being my thoughts, I naturally figured I could use that to my advantage. So, I started screaming at the top of my lungs. I yelled as loudly as I could possibly yell. I was attempting to instruct anyone who could hear me to come and help me! Call 911 – something! Surely with the thumping and blood curdling screams someone would jump into action. These walls were thin for crying out loud. I assumed that there was no way on earth the whole building couldn't have heard my cries for help.

But nobody came to my rescue... After what seemed to be thirty minutes of being a football finally ended, I was left crumpled on the floor, bleeding, bruised, and alone. Yet, I was thankful I still had breath in my body, but as I lay there, I took inventory of my body in order to determine if there were any broken bones. And I was again thankful that no bones were broken. It took me quite awhile to get my strength up to move, dust myself off, and resume my day – But I did.

When my roommate returned home, we called the police. While I was describing the incident so I could have charges pressed against Nathan, a young man came to my door and confessed that he was with Nathan during the knock-down, drag-out boxing match and witnessed everything. He also explained that he knew where Nathan was, and that he was only coming back to tell the police because Nathan was acting crazy and was harassing people in a nearby parking lot asking for money. The police followed him to the lot and arrested Nathan. Unfortunately for me, I was kind of baffled because I didn't see this young man at all during the beating. Apparently he was outside or something.

He Posted a Guard at My Door

The next morning, as I was walking down the sidewalk to go and get my mail out of my mailbox, I passed my neighbor's doorway at the same time as he was coming out. I took off my sunglasses and looked him right in the face.

"Didn't you hear me screaming for help yesterday?" I exclaimed as I stared him down! I wanted him to take a good long look at my face, but I will never forget the look of horror on his face.

As tears built up in his eyes, he raised his hands and said, "The guy at the door told me everything was all right, that it was just a game you two were playing inside."

Shaking my head, I looked straight into his eyes and said, "And you *believed* him?"

As he apologized profusely, it was obvious that he felt suckered, as he had been. I put my sunglasses back on my face and walked away. To this day my heart goes out to that man. I never knew his name, we never spoke again, but I can only imagine his agony over what he saw, and by knowing that he had every intention of helping me but got derailed by a strategically placed decoy, I'll bet you he has never missed another opportunity to help someone after that – or at least I hope not!

But, as it often is, justice can be blind. Later that afternoon, the police came back by my apartment and convinced me to drop the charges. They said having Nathan in jail would only make him angrier and that once he made bail, he would come back and take it out on me. Only after I had agreed to drop the charges out of fear of what the officers were telling me, did I realize that Nathan didn't have any bail money and neither did any of his friends! But, back in the early 1980s the domestic violence was not a high priority issue as it is today. I was made to feel that this incident was my fault and that the best thing to do would be to keep it quiet and not make any more waves. I guess this was another lesson on how to "hide my bruises…"

Another lesson that I learned was that once you have the knack for it, hiding your physical bruises can be very easy. And, if by chance someone did see a small bruise on me, I would simply explain how I "ran into a doorframe." *It's amazing how clumsy I* was *(wink-wink)!* As the old saying goes, "Humor covers a multitude of hurts."

All joking aside though, this is a huge issue that many of us may have faced, or are facing right now. Everyone at some point in his or her life puts on a mask of some sort. Sometimes we wear many masks. Sometimes, I think we have so many masks that we don't even know who we are underneath them all. It's no wonder that there are so many people walking around in so much confusion!

Thinking back on all of this makes me wonder about my own heart, today. What kind of "decoys" am I placing at my heart's door to keep people away from seeing the real me? Again, here is where those "masks" we so often wear come into play, because while I may be bleeding to death on the inside, I have posted a guard at my door to insure that nobody can see. Where is my faith? Where is my faith in the fact that there are those out there who want to help me and who can *help? Am I forcing those who try to come to my rescue to turn around and go back because they hear me say; "I'm fine?"*

I actually remember thinking that I couldn't take my masks off and become "normal" again after so many years of depression and anger. The person I had become is the person my friends and family knew. They didn't know the real me. I used to wonder about their reactions to me. I would often think, "What if they didn't like the real me? What if they think I'm being hypocritical?" I was forced to ask myself the question "Why all of a sudden am I happy and whole when all these years I've been so defeated?" I would even assume that my friends and family would also ask that same question of me, as well. See; it's much easier just to keep the mask on and continue living the defeated life. Why I thought my husband wouldn't actually like a happier, nicer wife is beyond me! And my kids, why wouldn't they want a more energetic and fun mother? What was I thinking?

Nevertheless, thinking back on the childhood "pictures" of what we thought our life was going to be like; how many of us can really say life worked out to be exactly the way we had planned? And still, no matter what life hands us, we try to act and live as if our life is exactly how we want it – perfect and F-I-N-E, fine! It's just like the ongoing joke that the word "FINE" stands for:

F-rantic;

I-nsecure;

N-eurotic; and,

E-motionally Disturbed!

So in a way, I suppose we are all "FINE" in one-way or another. Yet, why do we try to mold and form our life into being something it's not when our experiences and decisions play a huge part in shaping who we are? Instead of taking ownership of our failures, successes, and even our disappointments, we push that journey aside and insist that we are not going to allow them to affect how we want things to be. Nonetheless, by ignoring the consequences and life lessons that come with every decision we make leads us to an un-healthy viewpoint of ourselves. It is impossible to keep up a life that looks one way on the outside, but is another way on the inside. While we have the ability and control to decide how we are going react and grow from a circumstance, I think that more times than not, we choose to "disguise" our hurts and disappointments and act as if nothing has ever happened.

How about you? Do you hide behind a mask? What "bruises" are you hiding? I know we all have bruises and that we all wear masks, but now, the question is this: "Are we ready to take off our masks and un-cover our bruises and let others in who can help us heal?" **Jesus says, "Behold, I stand at the door and knock; if anyone hears my voice and opens the door, I will come into him and dine with him and he with me."** (Revelation 3:20, NAS) Do you hear the knocking?

My prayer for you, and for me, is that someday we can all open the door to friends, family, and God, and allow our real selves to shine through. Take off your masks, and let's save them just for masquerade parties...

❧Making Application in Your Life❧

Oftentimes things are not as they appear. People all around you everyday are hurting. Some people are hiding bruises that they hope no one will ever see. What are you accepting as reality? When someone says they are "fine" perhaps it's not enough to just smile and say, "That's great!" It just might be that there is a strategically placed guard at their heart.

As you walk through your day, take a look at two things; first, see if your own heart needs a changing of the guard. You may not be sporting a choir robe to hide your bruises, so what mask is it that you are using? Next time you interact with someone, be aware of your conversation. Are you passively saying you are "fine?" What is it you don't want them to know about you? Second, as you engage with other people slow down and read between the lines. Do they have guards placed at their heart's door? When we move past the pleasantries of the "Hi, how are you?" and the "I'm fine, thank you" – we can then begin to dialogue on a deeper level. It's in those deeper conversations that we become real with each other. Once we realize that someone genuinely cares and isn't judging us, we can begin an authentic relationship. Be that special someone today!

"People won't love you because you are perfect
They'll appreciate you because you are real."
Gina Parris

Chapter 13

That Darned Volkswagen

Like many people, I like to make my way to the kitchen every morning for a hot cup of tea or coffee. And like many apartment kitchens, there was a window above the sink looking out onto the parking lot. Not the view I would have preferred, but it's what I had. One particular morning, I made it to the kitchen still half asleep and looked out onto my wonderful view of black top and old junker cars. Nathan's "junker" was an old orange, square-back Volkswagen. I don't remember the year, but I do remember it was very loud. This particular morning, Nathan's car seemed a bit different. Long strands of grass and straw were sticking out from every nook and cranny and the driver's side window was smashed out.

Like any normal wife, I naturally ran back to the bedroom to find out what happened.

"What happened to your car?"

"What do you mean; what happened to my car?"

"Your car; the driver side window is smashed out. What happened?"

"Oh yea, I forgot!" He said as he grinned and snickered with a proud air about himself.

"Well?" I was waiting for the answer, should be a good one.

"I ran off the road and landed in a ditch," he said with a chuckle.

"What happened? Are you okay?" He obviously was just fine; it must have been more like an amusement ride to him.

"I don't remember, I think I was too stoned and I misjudged a corner." And that was that, he just rolled over and went back to sleep.

A few days later, once again during my morning ritual of tea drinking, I looked out at our "gorgeous" panoramic view of old cars parked on a sea of blacktop. My eyes stopped on the ugly orange square-back Volkswagen. It was difficult to really be sure; it had to be the early morning light, but this time I was quite certain the entire windshield was missing from the car.

"Now what happened?" I yelled. "Why is the windshield missing?"

"Oh man, it was so awesome! I rolled my car!"

"Were you drinking?" I asked.

"I was pretty wasted; I don't even remember how I got home." Again, Nathan was so proud and found the whole situation comical. He believed he had such a great adventure.

This went on a few more weeks, each time I found dents here or there, and windows cracked or missing. I just knew that one of these days he was going to be killed in a car accident. My mind wondered into a darker side as I thought about why I would need a divorce...after all, if I just wait long enough, I'll be a widow. I told myself that this was a much better solution than having a "sinful" divorce on my record. Like I said, I went to my dark place. However, I felt I had good reason to think this way because prior to our marriage, Nathan made a statement in front of our whole church one Sunday night. He said, "If I ever backslide again, I want the Lord to just take me home because it just isn't worth it." It was as if someone standing right behind me whispered into my ear, "I'm going to hold him to that." It was the Holy Spirit – and it was a little un-nerving. At that point I knew God either had something very big in mind for Nathan's life, or Nathan would have a hard road ahead of him if he kept straying away from God. Remembering what the Holy Spirit had whispered to me, I tried over and over to remind Nathan of his proclamation; begging him to stop the drugs and drinking. He didn't seem to care. It was only natural for me to think that he would be killed in a car accident or drug overdose...

Trigger Points & Very Loud Engines

If you have ever owned an older Volkswagen, or had the privilege of being a passenger in one, you will know what I mean when I say the engines are not quiet. If you ask me, they sound more like small airplane engines. After awhile, the sound of this engine became a very stressful sound. While it was good having the "heads up" that Nathan was just around the corner, it was also my clue that I would probably be getting more bruises.

Abusers usually have a pattern of being abusive one moment, then being apologetic and sweet the next. Nathan's pattern seemed to be every other visit; but really, it wasn't that predictable. After he moved out of the apartment, whenever I'd hear that roaring engine coming around the corner, my nerves would get so frazzled that I would end up in the bathroom vomiting. I wasn't really sure if he was coming to cause more trouble or to apologize for the trouble he caused earlier.

The days I had multiple visits were very exhausting days. The sheer mental and emotional games that were played on me only added to any physical violence, which would turn my stomach into knots.

It took me quite some time before I could play "slug bug" again after Nathan's death. This is one of those "trigger points" that I had to learn to deal with and to get over. If I let the sound of an old Volkswagen send me into a tailspin every time I heard it, I might as well never leave my home. We all have certain things that trigger memories, good and bad. Some triggers are so traumatic that it can actually invoke physical responses. At first, hearing another Volkswagen roaring by made me want to run to the nearest bathroom. I had to keep telling myself, "It's not Nathan, and you're okay." It's not an easy thing to do and many people never really deal with their own triggers.

Hiding my bruises while singing in the choir

*If you are someone that is dealing with something similar to this, I want to encourage you to **really** deal with it. Look it in the face and claim your life back; especially if it is something that you really enjoyed at one time. This can be a certain smell of a specific food, a sound or a song, even a place. It is not easy, but it is possible to enjoy the very thing that once brought so much pain. And now I can say that I am particularly fond of the new Volkswagen Bugs! Complete with a flower in the dashboard and all.*

A Surreal Moment

After Nathan's death, I would have one more encounter with this little orange square-back. It didn't even cross my mind that his car would be . . . somewhere. I didn't even know where his apartment was and I certainly wasn't wondering where that annoying little car was at. But one day as I was driving out from my apartment to do some errands, there it was sitting in a church parking lot. And why wouldn't it be? The field that Nathan took his life in was behind this church, right next to my apartment.

I must have driven by this parking lot fifty times since Nathan died. Why didn't I see the car before? But this time, as I was driving by, my eyes glanced over and there it was. It was all alone; the parking lot was empty. It was un-mistakenly there; as big as daylight and it took the breath right out of me. I gasped with the sudden realization that I now had to deal with getting this car home.

Pulling into the parking lot, my mind was racing. Fear filled my very being as I pulled up and parked beside the abandoned car. All I could think about were some of those last words Nathan had spoken to me. Phrases like: "If I can't have you, nobody can have you." "Without me, you will never be happy." I especially heard the words of the fire marshal when he told me the night of the fire that I was very lucky I was not home alone. He was pretty certain had I been alone, Nathan would have killed himself along with the baby and me. My imagination went wild. Would Nathan really have tried to plot my death even after his own? As I got out of my car and walked towards the abandoned Volkswagen, my throat became dry and my heart felt very heavy. I had my keys in my hand but I couldn't bring myself to start the engine. Maybe I watch too many movies, but the thought of dynamite exploding as I turned the ignition was very vivid in my mind.

What seemed like hours of just standing there in total shock and fear looking at this car was really about 15 minutes. I was relieved when a police officer pulled into the parking lot.

"Do you know something about this car?" The officer asked.

"Yes, I do. I guess it's mine now. It was my husband's car," I flatly replied.

"We've been trying to figure out who this car belonged to." Does this have anything to do with the suicide that occurred here a few days ago?" He asked.

"Yes. He must have parked it here. I didn't even see it until now. I don't know what to do." I began to shake as I fought back the tears.

I proceeded to tell him my fear of starting the car and why. The officer was very kind and helpful. He asked if I wanted help getting it home. When I told him I just had to get it next door to my apartment, he offered to drive it for me himself. I was still hesitant – I didn't want the nice officer to die in the explosion! He was very careful to check underneath the car, all the tires, and the gas tank. We decided to go ahead and look at the engine, just in case. Now, remember, engines in old Volkswagens are in the back of the vehicle. As we lifted the hatch to get to the engine, there were a couple more surprises for me. There laid nicely across the back were Nathan's coat, keys, and wallet. First of all, I was amazed they were still there since the car had been unlocked. WOW. Talk about a surreal moment. The officer asked me if this was his stuff as we looked through everything. I searched through the pockets of the jacket hoping to find some sort of note. But there was no note, just his coat, his keys, and his wallet. Everything was in place from his driver's license to photos of me and our baby. These items were not just in the car by mistake; they were intentionally placed there in a neat and systematic manner. It was almost like a respectful goodbye to let me know that yes, Nathan meant to do this.

There are no words that can describe what I was feeling at that moment. Even as I write this, I have a lump in my throat and that surreal feeling is so fresh in my mind.

The officer started the car and drove it around and parked it in a spot behind my apartment. We felt it would be better if it were not the first thing I saw everyday when I looked out my kitchen window. As far as the coat, keys, and wallet, the officer had to take them as evidence while they were investigating the case. I felt like I was in some kind of dramatic movie. I did eventually get those items back. I was also able to sell the car to my neighbor. I'm still trying to figure out how that happened, but it was good to get rid of that car, and it was definitely time to start looking for a new place to live. The sooner the better!

❧Making Application in Your Life☙

Do you find yourself struggling with trigger points from experiences in your past? Do you even recognize that you have trigger points? Are there moments in your life when out of nowhere you are suddenly feeling anxious, annoyed, or even terrified? Chances are you are subconsciously, or even knowingly, experiencing something that is triggering a bad memory or event that has taken place in your life. Is there a certain phrase, or a smell for you, or maybe even being a place that brings back familiarity or a feeling of being there before? These things can be overcome. It's not easy, but with a lot of fortitude you can press on.

I encourage you take a long hard look at your life. Make a list every time you start to feel overwhelmed or anxious and you don't know why. Make a note about what you were doing and where you were at during those times. What phrases did you hear? What was the atmosphere like? Over time, you will begin to see a pattern of what your trigger points are. If need be, seek professional counseling as a way to start overcoming the things you are hanging onto. Pray! Get into God's word and receive the redemption and healing that is offered to you through God's son, Jesus Christ. It's not an easy road to walk. Believe me; I know how much easier it seems to just stay in a state of depression or unhappiness. It seems effortless. BUT, life is worth the living!

You are not called to live in bondage. I encourage you to take your life back! Look those trigger points right in the face and rise above them! You can do it! I know you can. Because, believe me, if I can do it, anybody can!

Chapter 14

Dear Prozac, Thank You!

"Yeah, I'll go. What can it hurt? Nothing else seems to be working."

When I finally gave into the idea of going to see a psychologist I was desperate and at my wits end. For months, I had tried to apply the principles of the Bible and live a life of joy. On the inside, my heart was joyful, and I longed to laugh and love. But, no matter what I did, the happiness I was feeling in my heart could not turn into any outward expression. It was very frustrating.

As I shared my two conflicting worlds with Dr. G, he seemed to know what I was trying to express. There was a big door that was locked and on one side was happiness and joy and on the other side was dry and baron land; very quiet and extremely lonely. I could not get the door open to happiness even though my life depended on it. My heart and attitude was on the side that had the joy, and my physical being was on the other side; trapped.

After taking a very long and comprehensive test that had hundreds and hundreds of questions, Dr. G proceeded to tell me why I was struggling with these two worlds. The simple version; my nervous system was literally frozen. As in, no matter what emotion I felt in my heart or on the inside, there was no possible way those emotions could break through the surface and show on my face, or in my actions.

What's Up Doc?

The test I took was to determine if I had Post Traumatic Stress Disorder (PTSD). Who would have thought that I had some type of "disorder" relating to traumatic situations? Whatever would have brought that on? *Yes, my quirkiness is often laced with sarcasm…*

As soon as the word "Prozac" came out of Dr. G's mouth, I immediately suited-up to play defense.

"No way; I'm not going on Prozac!"
I didn't want to seem ungrateful, but Dr. G was asking me to do something that was very frowned upon. "I'm a pastor's wife for crying out loud. I can't take Prozac!"

Dr. G was very kind and very gracious. He continued to explain that without it, my nervous system would stay frozen. Prozac was the only way to get my body jump started again.

"Give me one year. I promise you will only be on this medication for one year and I promise you won't become addicted to it," he said.

I looked over at my husband and he nodded lovingly to me. "Yes, honey, you need to do this. It's time." Somehow, I found it within myself to agree and follow the treatment Dr. G was prescribing.

Hiding my bruises while singing in the choir

It turned out Dr. G was correct. One year was all I needed. I did not become addicted and the change was pretty immediate.

It's not Normal to Explode over Spilled Milk?

Scene One:

KIDS: "Daddy, is Mommy sick?"

HUSBAND: "No Honey, why do you ask?"

KIDS: "She didn't get angry when we spilled the milk."

What we get from our kids...

In the pre-Prozac me, I got angry over spilled milk *(and many other things)* but on this particular occasion, I did not get angry. The kids were playing around with a glass of milk. Seeing what was about to unfold, I said, "You better stop or you're going to . . ." Just at that moment, even before I could finish my sentence, milk flew everywhere. As the kids tensed up in preparation for my wrath, I began to laugh. As I threw them each a towel I said, "Have fun cleaning it up!" Still chuckling, I turned and went into my bedroom for my nightly routine of getting ready for bed, thinking how awesome it was to see the kids interacting, and playing around together. A few moments later, Doug came into the room and told me about the scene that started this chapter.

He answered the kids, "No, mommy was sick, but now she's getting better."

My heart both broke and rejoiced, all in the same beat. I saw the horrified anticipation on their faces when they spilled the milk. They were very familiar with the drill. But this time my reaction was very unexpected, and to their amazement, I was actually laughing "with" them, not yelling "at" them. How sad to think that this change in behavior made them question my health. My heart broke because my kids thought it to be "normal" that I would go through the roof over spilled milk. But I also rejoiced as I recognized the healing process was beginning and I had hope for the first time in many, many years.

I can't believe I allowed such anger and depression to take over my life for so long. For thirteen years I kept telling myself that God was my healer, therefore I didn't need to go to counseling. *I wasn't depressed; this is just how I am now* – my new mantra. After all, I did experience some pretty traumatic things. I thought I was entitled to be angry, since it's much easier to be depressed and angry. Otherwise, I might have to admit that I needed help and fight for some kind of "normalcy" in life. Quite frankly, it took way too much energy to be happy. The times I tried to be happy, things would just fall apart again. Situation after situation, one more thing after another, pretty soon I felt like I was going to explode! I was on the bottom of a junk pile and it was getting higher and higher burying me in disappointment and sucking the breath of life right out of me. Something had to give because at that point something as light as a feather would have sent me right over the edge. I was done. Totally exhausted and spent.

Hiding my bruises while singing in the choir

So you see, this was a huge step in my journey back to "happy." It only took me thirteen years to finally see how I was allowing depression and anger to rule my world. Unfortunately, those were also our child-raising years. I wasn't at all the mother I intended to be during all those years of playing "house" and loving on my baby dolls.

Washington My Home, Wherever I May Roam!

I felt such a huge improvement in just a few days after starting on the Prozac. For the first time in years, I could think beyond just a few minutes. I remember when I made a statement that included the words; "next week" - I actually stopped and had to think about that. "Next week." WOW! I could see beyond that moment and actually plan and think ahead. When you are depressed, it's all you can do to live moment to moment. If anyone asks what your plans are for the weekend or the following holiday, it's like asking someone where exactly they will be in fifty years. Who the heck knows?

A couple of months after starting the medication I began to feel really homesick for my hometown of Spokane, WA. Every memory and all the people from Spokane gave me happy thoughts. I had been living in such darkness for so long that I wanted to just leave it behind and go some place I knew would make me feel complete again. I wasn't sure what Dr. G would say about that, but Doug and I agreed it would be a good idea and we would ask him at our next visit.

When we spoke to Dr. G, he asked how things were going. I told him they were going great; however, there was one little issue I wanted to talk to him about. Shaking his head, Dr. G proceeded to tell us he forgot to mention the possible side effects that can inhibit the sexual relationship. HA! *Wow, didn't expect that one.* Fortunately for me, that was NOT one of the side effects I was experiencing. After we stopped laughing, at his assumption, we began to discuss the possibility of my returning to home.

Dr. G asked me about my motivations and my reasoning. He talked to my husband about how he felt as well. After determining that I was not "running" from my problems, but indeed was trying to "move on," Dr. G gave us his approval and blessing to move home to Spokane. He felt it would be very helpful in my recovery. It is important for you, the reader, to realize that on any given day I was passing the very spot that Nathan committed suicide 4-6 times a day. My work was just a block down the street. Our church was a couple blocks down the street. The mall and various businesses we frequented were all in the same area. I wasn't trying to "run" by going home. I needed to change my surroundings so I could heal better.

We ended up landing in Coeur d'Alene, Idaho just next to Spokane. In those ten years I slowly started regaining my life back one baby step at a time. Being surrounded by the familiarity of my childhood and good memories, seemed to be just the ticket I needed. I'm so thankful for that time of retreat and healing.

The funny thing is . . . we are back living in Oregon now. *Didn't see that one coming!* At first, there were many challenges and "triggers" associated with being back in Oregon, but God has been so gracious and faithful, I'm walking through even more of the healing process and growing in ways I never thought possible.

We never know where our path is going to lead on this journey of life. Sometimes the detours can be beautiful and sometimes they can be life altering in traumatic ways. Either way, we need to remember that we always have the capacity to keep moving forward on the path of life. We choose if we are going to "camp" and focus only on one thing or if we will keep walking and embrace the growth that comes with living life! Count your blessings, not your burdens! Jesus has come to set us free and give us life. An abundant life at that! And once in awhile, if you need a friend like "Prozac" to help you get back on track . . . then I say good for you for recognizing you are "stuck" and need a little help!

If I say, "No," You Won't Die

I shared already that I had three deaths of people who were close to me and played important roles in my life: Father, grandfather, and husband. Their deaths all occurred within four years of each other and each took a piece of my heart with them.

Dealing with death had become such a part of my routine that whenever Doug was fifteen minutes late, I was sure he was lying on the side of the road somewhere dead. I had it all played out in my mind. The police officer would come to my door to deliver the news and I knew whom I would have to call and what I would have to say. Funeral arrangements would be going through my head. My inner strength would rise up as I processed life as a widow . . . again. I know its crazy – but it's what I did. You can probably imagine the relief that flooded my soul when my husband walked through the door or called.

Post Traumatic Stress Disorder is such a life limiting disability. For me, it kept those around me and myself from experiencing life because of the fear of death. *Death is the opposite of Life. Do our fears "cripple" us? You bet they do!*

I had this need to have complete control of everything and everyone around me. Having control made me feel safe; it also made me feel like I was protecting those around me. When my kids asked if they could go play at the park, I would first have to run through my mind all the potential dangerous scenarios that could be lurking there. Of course, my imagination was very active and I think I conjured up situations that aren't even possible! But nonetheless, my fear of having one more loved one die kept limitations on the fun they could have in their lives. How horrible for my little kids. I'm sure they just thought I was being mean or

Hiding my bruises while singing in the choir

being lazy. Don't get me wrong, we did go to the park many times. We just played it very safe!

When I think back on all the times I squashed the fun for my kids out of my fear, it makes me cringe! The mother I became was not at all the mother I imagined I would be. One of my biggest dreams as a little girl was growing up to be the best mommy there ever was! How devastating it is that I became just the opposite.

But there is hope and there is redemption through Jesus Christ. It's there for the taking if you just ask.

❧Making Application in Your Life☙

So, how are you doing? Are you F.I.N.E.? (Frantic, insecure, neurotic, and emotionally disturbed) If you're like me and had the upbringing that using an antidepressant is not the Christian thing to do, then I have great news for you! IT'S A LIE! Believe me I know what I'm talking about! I spent over ten years in depression based on the fact premise that I was not allowed to find "prescription" relief as a Christian. My body was frozen – shut down – not functioning. And God chose to use modern medicine to get my body going again. Sure, He could have healed me; of course He had that option! But for some reason, he allowed me to walk this journey and brought me to a place of realization that receiving help form a counselor and even medications was OK.

Pride is very overrated....

But, I know that pride is one of the main factors that keeps us from seeking the help we need, and I say, "Get rid of it!" Pride has no place in your life! There is nothing wrong with admitting we need help or that we have failed. God is there to pick you back up and set you back on your feet. Allow the Holy Spirit to direct you. Claim the promises of God and his redemption. He sees no stain on you for you are his bride. He loves you beyond any love we can comprehend. Don't miss out on the blessings He has for you. If you stay "stuck" you miss out on so much life, and we were put on this earth to live in God's light and not in darkness.

Chapter 15

All My Clothes Are Shrinking

Have you ever struggled with your weight? Loaded question I know, what Westernized woman hasn't? With all the messages we receive from the media, there is a certain image we feel we have to personify. Growing up, I never struggled with weight issues. I was always slim and a healthy size 7. I ate what I wanted and when I wanted, and my activities must have been enough to burn through the calories I had consumed. I never had to worry about my weight, and nor did I strive to be a different size. But as so many women do, I hit a moment in my life when my weight was at its highest and I didn't like what I saw.

The Weight Battle Begins

As you know, my freshman year of college I was faced with an unplanned pregnancy. Of course it was unplanned; After all, I was in Bible College and eighteen years-old preparing to become the perfect pastor's wife! *Funny how life is, huh?* Well, it's either funny, or it is just that the sins of our youth will eventually find us out!

I weighed 105 pounds when I married Nathan. But, morning sickness got the best of me! During my pregnancy, Nathan wanted to insure the baby would be healthy, so he began monitoring my food intake. I was told what I could eat, when I could eat it, and how much I could eat. If sugar was an ingredient, it **did not** go into my mouth. Since I'm a confirmed chocoholic, this was extremely torturous! Finally, when I did get to enjoy one square of a Hershey's Chocolate Bar, it was due to my mom's intervention. (Thanks mom!) *Let me tell you, that was one savored piece of chocolate!* After the baby was born, the control over what I ate became even more rigid because I was nursing, and Nathan didn't want a fat wife!

For some reason, probably stress, I wasn't producing enough milk to keep the baby fully satisfied, even though it seemed as if she was eating every hour! Baby formula was not allowed in the house. Nathan was very adamant about that – to the point he would sit and watch me during the feeding to make sure I wasn't using a bottle. Again, it was my mom's intercession that saved me. After Nathan went to work one day, she came over and helped me get some formula for the baby. Everyday, I would wait for him to leave, so I could give the bottle of formula to my baby. One day, however, he had forgotten something and ended up coming back home right at the moment I began using the bottle. I'll spare you the gory details! But in short, amid violence and threats, he threw away the bottle. A few months later, Nathan moved out for the final time.

Surviving on My Own... Now what do I eat?

W.I.C. (Women, Infants and Children) If you're not familiar with W.I.C., it's a program that provides baby formula and baby food; dairy products such as milk, eggs, cheese; and other items like cereal and peanut butter. The government provides this service to low income families or single moms. Every week, I would go and sit with other women through an educational class on nutrition, and at the end of it, we were given our vouchers. Oh thank heaven for such programs! For almost six months, my diet consisted of grilled cheese sandwiches, scrambles eggs, and peanut butter on toast. Needless to say, I fit back into those size 5 jeans pretty much the day after I gave birth, and I stayed there! It wasn't until people started noticing that perhaps I didn't have a whole lot of food in my cupboards, that a bigger change took place.

"The Change" started with my sister. During one of her visits, she wanted to make me lunch. After a short time in the kitchen, she asked, "Janice, what do you eat?"

"Toast and peanut butter or grilled cheese" I replied.

"Every day?" she inquired.

"No," I proclaimed, "Sometimes scrambled eggs and cheese!" After a trip to the grocery store and a lecture on the importance of vegetables in one's diet, my sister proceeded to make the largest batch of vegetable beef soup that I had ever seen!

Hiding my bruises while singing in the choir

"There", she said, "This should last you for awhile!" And it did.

Then my roommate and college friends joined the cause of "Making Sure Jan has Food!" They would all chip-in to fill my cupboards with food and make sure I licked my plate clean. I found myself hungrier and hungrier all the time. Food became my newfound joy in life! It was not uncommon for me to eat at McDonalds and polish off two Big Macs, a super sized fry, a couple rounds of pop, and an apple pie for dessert. And yes, all **in one** sitting! Oh, and by that time, if my kids, Jaylene and Jeremy, didn't finish their meals, I'd come to their rescue and finish their meals, too!

I went from 105 pounds to 210 pounds in 1 ½ years! I was up seven sizes! I went from a size 5 to size 20/22. My pendulum had swung from one extreme to the other. Here begins my struggle with my weight for the first time in my life. Food ultimately became my emotional comforter, because I would use food as a way to cope with my pain. When I felt sad; I'd eat. When I felt happy; I'd eat. When I was bored; I'd eat! When I felt I had no control over a situation; I'd eat. *If you're into technical terms, you would call this "Emotional Eating!"*

Thirteen years went by and nothing was improving. I was a size 20/22 and I was depressed, unhappy, angry, and bitter. I hated myself and couldn't stand to look in the mirror! I kept telling myself that I had been skinner longer than I have been fat, and as long as I get it off before that flips, I'd be okay. In my mind's eye, I still saw the "skinny" me. I was in denial about how big I was. *We see what we want to believe, don't we?* But photos do not lie! With each one of them, there it was right in front of me in living color – I was huge! I looked unhappy and I was appalled!

Controlled by a Dead Man

As I was sitting and reflecting one day, I asked myself why I was so unhappy when God had been so faithful to me. Why was I allowing myself to be fat and depressed? And it hit me! In all this time, I still had not completely dealt with the turn of events that had resulted in Nathan's death. Not only had I *not* dealt with them, but the words he had spoke to me over and over were still resonating in my head. I was still being controlled by a dead man! Too many times I heard:

"You will never be happy without me."

"If I can't have you, no one else can have you either."

"I will be there to stop any happiness you try and have."

Those words were controlling my life, and the power of those statements somehow stuck to me like glue. And it was true. I was not happy.

I asked myself, "Why am I letting a dead man control me?" This became my "light bulb" moment. I was living out Nathan's words, just like they were a prophecy, by not allowing myself to be happy.

Hiding my bruises while singing in the choir

"Not anymore," I proclaimed!

From that moment forward, I began to take my life back from the grave. I took a "no excuse" approach and worked-out at the gym four nights a week. I also followed a sound-eating program that taught me how to properly nourish my body. Within two years, I successfully lost 45 pounds and 5 dress sizes.

On my 40th birthday, I was a size 10! It was so gratifying to hear the Doctor say that I had reached my healthy weight. I did it! I took my life back! Had I waited one more year, I would have been fat longer than I had been skinny. It was a mental issue for me, and I felt victorious in my accomplishment.

&Making Application in Your Life&

What influences affect the way you treat your own body? Are you controlled by the words of the media and the picture-perfect models that are splashed on every ad and every magazine cover? Has someone spoken harsh words to you that keep repeating over and over in your head? You don't have to take those words or those images as truth. The TRUTH is that you have the ability to resurrect your healthy self. I encourage you to ask yourself, "What are the words in my life that are limiting me from being who I am destined to be?" Do you hear words like failure, fear, disappointing, embarrassment, shame, and guilt? Write them down and ask God to take their power away. Again, I challenge you to take your life back from whatever "grave" is holding you down!

Repeat after me...

"I am important and worth the effort to be my best."

"Happiness is a choice (a choice to do the work to be happy) and I choose to be happy."

"God loves me and is for me; who then can be against me?"

"I chose what I allow to influence me. I don't have to receive hurtful words as truth."

Feel better now?   Good!

See you at the gym or the produce aisle!

Chapter 16

I Like Happy Endings, Don't You?

At the date of this writing, (2011), Doug and I have been married for 27 years. We are empty nesters and enjoying life!

Doug is completing his dissertation; he graduates in Spring of 2012. He is a co-founder, along with me, of Red Couch Coaching where he serves as a pastoral counselor and leadership consultant. He leads a conversational Bible study in our home every week; it's called "The Community Couch."

Jaylene is now 28, married to her high school sweet heart, and together they have four beautiful children. Chloe is 9, almost 10. Jacosa is 8. Kyle is 3, and Jonah is 1 ½. I call their family the Johnson Six. I call my grandkids the "Fabulous Four." And the best part . . . they live just down the street from us! She is an amazing mother, wife, and friend. Jeff, her husband, has a fabulous job and is a wonderful husband, father, and provider. As a family, they are very committed to Christ and are involved in many community projects. I'm so very proud of them.

Jeremy is now 26 and attending college in California. He is studying Japanese. He just completed a five year term with the Marines. He served in Iraq for a year. He is extremely artistic and creative. He has his father's mind – he loves to learn and research his topics of interest. He has his mother's humor – he is quick witted and kind hearted. I'd say he got the best of both worlds! I'm so very proud of the man he is becoming.

As for me, I am a life coach at Red Couch Coaching; specializing in Hope Coaching. Helping others to emerge from their broken dreams and encouraging them to choose to move forward in life.

I'm so very thankful for my life and family. Do I struggle still with the first part of my "movie?" YES! Absolutely I do, sometimes on a daily basis. But I've learned the difference between living like a defeated victim and being an over comer living in Joy, Redemption, and Hope! When I look back at my life, I have a choice. I can be bitter, angry, and disappointed OR, I can be redeemed, thankful, and productive. I take it one day at a time, just like everyone else. I have my dark days and my bright days. But always, my days are a gift and I want to live life to the fullest.

I still love to sing and walk along side my husband in ministry. And if you couldn't tell, I love movies! But no gory, shoot em up type movies . . . mostly the romantic comedy sappy movies that make me laugh and cry. I love spending time with family and friends, eating, playing table games, watching movies, or just chatting at a coffee house!

Over all, I'd say I'm pretty normal, whatever normal is.

Section Three
Insights, Facts, & Resources

Chapter 17

Our Perception is Our Reality

It's really hard for me to understand how people can "settle" into life and think that it's going to be "this way" forever. Life is a verb—and a living journey. We don't know from day-to-day or even hour to hour what turns may appear on the road of life. When we marry the person of our dreams, we have an expectation that they will remain exactly as they are forever. We don't take into account the aging process, the learning curve, or the overall factors that mold and shape us, such as traumatic situations. Every little experience we go through adds something new to our life. Losing a loved one through death or divorce leaves a huge void, or scar, on your heart. If you think over the past five years of your life, try to count the "life changing" events you have experienced. Moving, changing jobs, death of a loved one, divorce, falling in love, drama of friends and family members . . . the list goes on. Nobody can walk through life and these kinds of situations and not grow/change to adapt to each "new thing."

I've only experienced one major panic attack where I felt the walls were literally falling in on me. Catching a breath was next to impossible, and I felt suffocation was surely going to be the way I exited this world. Job stress had been piling higher and higher on my plate and I was really feeling it. As I was walking through trying to cope with all the stress, I noticed that my good friend, and co-worker, was pulling away from me. When I asked her about it, she replied, "You're not the Jan I know – You're changing." I tried to reassure her that I was the SAME Jan she knows; only now, she's seeing a side that she had never seen before. Because I'm always so happy and full of life, seeing me stressed and unhappy was foreign to her. Instead of walking alongside me and helping me to walk through my difficult season, like so many of us do, she pulled away and assumed I changed and she'd never see the "happy" Jan again. I explained that we all have many sides – and we all walk through many things that we can't always predict, we can never know how our emotions will make us react at every instance. We were able to continue our friendship and still do even to this day. She is a blessing to me, but this was also a lesson learned.

Expectations are dangerous. When we put our expectations onto someone else and insist they have to follow through with what we want rather than supporting what they want, we lose a piece of ourselves, by projecting ourselves on another. Our feelings, perceptions, and expectations are our own—regardless if others feel they are right or wrong. Our reality is and always will be our own reality. We can't assign our own feelings and realities onto someone else. As we walk through life and grow with each situation, our realities and perceptions change as we adapt and gain wisdom and experience.

"Doing life intentionally" is one of my mottos. Anytime I can do "life" for the sake of others, I find my life has more purpose and function than if I just live for "myself." When I think through just one of my days where every phone call delivers bad news and one thing after the other goes wrong and it's not exactly good timing financially; I have to wonder how many other people are walking around with me that are feeling the same pressures or walking through their own situations. It becomes so much easier to slow down and let someone in the lane ahead of you. It gives me so much more compassion as a person to see someone standing behind me in the grocery line who has two or three items vs. my heaping cart to say, "Why don't you go ahead of me, I don't want to hold you up." Even just sharing a happy smile and a friendly hello can make a world of difference in someone's life. I try to spark a conversation everywhere I go. My favorite conversations are with those people who look so stressed and overwhelmed, but after a brief exchange of words, they end up laughing or smiling. *My perfect dream job is. . . making people feel happy or important or needed . . .anybody know of any open positions in this field?*

Words, Phrases, & Other Misnomers

Have you ever heard any of these phrases?

"There must be sin in your life if you're so sick."

"Jesus is the only one that can and will heal you."

"If you are on antidepressants, you're not trusting God."

"Seeking professional counseling is not something Christians do."

"Divorce is never an option; especially if you are a Christian."

"You just keep praying for him dear, he will come to Jesus one of these days."

These are just a small handful of the "Christian Phrases" that have been floating around for years. If you think about it, I'm sure you could easily add to this list. My point is that even if there is some truth within each of these quotes, they cannot be so staunch and rigid that there is no room for grace. There is a reason that Paul warned us, ***"Not of letter but of spirit; for the letter kills, but the Spirit gives life" (2 Corinthians 3:6b).*** Even truth taken out of context can bring death. Different people along the way spoke those well-meaning phrases to me. Ironically, those words are what kept me from seeking the help I so desperately needed. When I think about those thirteen years of suffering and pain, my stomach gets into knots. We're not supposed to dwell on the "What ifs" but . . . WHAT IF I had been courageous enough to seek the help I needed rather than stand upon the "truth" of these phrases that were ingrained in me at a very young age?

Perhaps I would not have run back to Nathan ten times only to get beaten up each time worse than the time before. All that abuse, because I was feeling guilty over the word "divorce." What if I had sought professional counseling within the first year of Nathan's death? For some reason I was determined that if I just waited and was patient, God would eventually come through for me and take all the pain away. When I found out that antidepressants were not "of the devil," I was kind of miffed that I squandered away so many years of my life. I could have been that "mommy" I so wanted to be...

But like I said, we can't dwell on the "what ifs."

What we can focus on however, is the way we allow our circumstances to determine the quality of our life right now. There are always consequences to our actions or choices. Some choices have consequences that are small and over with quickly. Others stay with us throughout our entire life. The good news is we have the choice to determine which mindset we have towards the things we chose to allow into our lives. We can choose bitterness and depression, or the path that leads to healing. My choices were ones that changed my life forever. If we look hard enough, we can always find the good in a situation. In my case, my beautiful daughter was the beginning to having a wonderful family that has now expanded into having four of most wonderful grandchildren.

Are you stagnant or growing?

Self imposed boundaries and negative self-talk is HUGE! Most of us do not even realize that we have checked out of life and allowed the "words" of others to form who we are. Ask someone if they can remember a time somebody made them feel stupid or unworthy and they will most likely have not one, but many occasions they could tell you about. Does that make it true? NO! It's a feeling or a perception we walked away with after the event happened. So what do we do with this?

We are either growing or we are decaying. *This is according to Plato, and I agree whole-heartedly!* When did life get reduced down to something we have no control over? What happens to a plant if it doesn't receive water and the proper lighting required? What happens to a body of water that has no movement? The plant withers and dies and the body of water becomes stinky and full of "stuff" like bacteria, algae, and icky bugs. The plant dies while the water is still alive, but who wants to swim in it? For some reason, we can get to a place in life where we accept it as it is and figure we can't do or have anything more. Are we moving forward with that kind of mindset? And what happens when we don't keep things moving forward? We either wither and die or become stagnant. Either way, neither of those two outcomes is pleasant to think about.

This carries over into our relationships more than we know. Think about it. Have you ever tried to keep someone acting or being the "same" as always! What happens when their behavior or beliefs start to change as a result of their own growth? We tend to not like it too much.

How about theses phrases; have you heard or used any of these in your lifetime?

"You're not the same person you were when I met you!"

"You're acting differently ever since 'that' happened to you!" (Whatever "that" may be)

"I don't know you anymore!"

"Who are you and what have you done with my friend?"

"We used to be on the same page!"

"I can't figure you out!"

I could go on and on with these types of statements as well. Have you ever said anything like this to someone? Has someone said it to you? GOOD! That means there is growth in process. It cracks me up that when we get married; many of us truly believe that our spouse will be in the same mindset or the same place 10 years, 20, years, or even 30 years down the road. I got married at 18. Does my spouse really want me to act and be like I was when I was 18 when I'm 45 or 50? Probably not, but in reality, don't we have that expectation? We don't go into a relationship with the mindset that we are agreeing to take a journey together and there will be events in our life that will continue to mold and shape us; that our beliefs change as the facts change; as we learn more, we adapt to other possibilities more. Rather, I think we are starting a journey with the person we love right now – and that's how it will always be – a journey. Love isn't supposed to be like putting somebody in a box and saying, "You can never experience growth."

Another phrase often spoken to a loved one is "We've grown so far apart." Is it that you've grown apart, or that one of you is growing and the other one is not? It is important that both people are constantly growing and becoming who they are. It's not about the other person being who you want them to be, but loving them for who they are now and as they develop.

If we do not allow room for growth in each other and in ourselves, we reduce others and ourselves to being just an object. Objects are not alive so they can't die or grow stagnant.

I take so much joy in watching our grandchildren grow and discover things. It's incredible to think of all the possibilities they have in life. When does that childlike living stop? Why does that child-like living stop? I'm talking about the curiosity, the acceptance, the joy and love, and the boldness to explore.

Matthew 18:1-5 states, *"At that time the disciples came to Jesus and asked, "Who is the greatest in the kingdom of heaven? He called a little child and had him stand among them. And he said: "I tell you the truth, unless you change and become like little children, you will never enter the kingdom of heaven. Therefore, whoever humbles himself like this child is the greatest in the kingdom of heaven. And whoever welcomes a little child like this in my name welcomes me."*

Was Jesus saying that we stop growing when we lose that childlike outlook on life? It's something to think about and discover. Faith of a mustard seed, faith of a child; it seems like we try to make things too big in life. All we need is a little faith and a little curiosity. We all need to live intentionally in order to find our purpose and become the person God created us to be. So, again, I ask you to think about the words or phrases that have been spoken over you in life. At what point did they become truth for you and how long have you been operating with that truth? But more importantly, was it really the truth, or was it someone's opinion that you took on as your truth? It's time to do some purging. It's never too late to discover new truths and explore who you are.

⊷Making Application in Your Life⊷

I'm pretty sure we have all had hurtful words spoken to us. But, I've also come to understand that it's not the actual words themselves that impact us as much as it is the value we give to those words. When someone says to you, "You're so stupid," what is your initial reaction? Do you take in those words and believe it as truth, or do you spare your hurt feelings, set them aside, and say, "That's a lie; I'm not stupid; that is just your opinion." We have the opportunity to place value on the things that are said to us. We assign those words a place in our lives. Where are you allowing hurtful words to be in your life? If you give them value and attach meaning to them, then they will become reality in your world. If you are what you eat, then I'm pretty sure you are what you think! So, why are you thinking that others have the "say-so" in telling you who and what you are and what you can do? They are only words and opinions of others. What really matters are the words and opinions of Jesus Christ. He does not condemn you or tell you that you're a failure. He only offers words of life and healing. The word of God is the only true guidebook that shows us that there is hope, healing, love, compassion, joy, and peace . . . I could go on and on and on!

Get a piece of paper. Write down some very specific phrases that have been spoken over you that have crippled your confidence. Look at each situation. Evaluate the facts. How old where you, what was the circumstance? How did it impact you and why? Now, take that same list and turn each of those statements into a positive one. Overwrite what was written. Recognize that the person who spoke those words has no power over you. Only you can determine what the "truth" of your life is and what is not. Practice accepting yourself, and give yourself permission to mess up once in awhile. It's okay, we all mess up! We get up, dust our boots off, and keep walking!

Repeat after me...

"I am a child of God, made perfect in His image, and if I mess up, God forgives me. Therefore, I will forgive myself. I let go of the things that have crippled me and held me back in life. I release my fears and walk boldly in faith. With God's help, I will be made whole."

Chapter 18

Shattered Photographs

I think everyone had some sort of vision for their life when they were growing up. As small children we dream about what we want to be, what our family will look like, our home, the car we will drive. We begin to draw pictures of what our life will look like as an adult.

The pictures that we are forming start to set the tone of who we are and who we want to become. Combine those future pictures with our current circumstances, and we can see how our life and its surroundings begin to shape and mold us. For me, my childhood was very secure and happy. I was surrounded by lots of family and friends so my confidence was very high. My family was very involved in our church, so I had a strong faith as well as a good home life.

I will be the first to admit that I was pretty sheltered growing up. I was even naïve enough to suppose that everyone had that same security and love that I did! Looking back, I am amazed at how clueless I was to the pain and suffering that was going on all around me. I was so confident that I actually thought I had complete control over everything in my life! And that nothing could ever go wrong! How could it? Everyone loved me, life was good, and I had God, too! Can't get any better than that!

My pictures growing up were very specific. *As I'm sure yours were too.* I knew at the age of seven I wanted to be a pastor's wife. I knew I would be musical; I would have two children, a girl and a boy. I wanted a big house on a corner lot, and when mini-vans came onto the scene, I wanted one of those, too. Yes, life was going to be grand and I couldn't wait!

I can assure you that my "pictures" did NOT resemble any of the following:

- At 15 years of age, my dad would die of cancer

- In my junior year of high school, we would move to another state to take care of my ill grandfather

- At 16 years of age, I would meet the boy of my dreams (well – maybe this one was in my mind)

- At 17 years of age, my grandfather would die

- At 18 years of age, I would get pregnant and marry the boy of my dreams

- At 19 years of age, after a season of being physically & emotionally abused, my husband would commit suicide – and wait for me to watch.

Who in their right mind would ever imagine these sorts of things for their life? NOBODY! But this is how my "movie" ended up playing out. And it crushed me so low I felt I had to look up to see the belly of an ant. The next fifteen years were spent trying to pick up the pieces while maintaining some sort of

Hiding my bruises while singing in the choir

"normalcy" in life. Depression, anger, and fear loomed very heavy over me and I had never experienced any of this before. I was in a foreign land.

The Editing Room

We all picture what we want our life to look like. So, what happens when those pictures, like mine, don't make the cut? They end up on the floor in the editing room. And our life is somehow playing something unfamiliar and unreal. Can we still enjoy the movie?

Sometimes we get so wrapped up in what has gone wrong in our lives that we fail to see what is going right. God has a way of slipping in blessings and giving us the desires of our heart even in the midst of crisis. All along while I was struggling with my life in ruins, God was quietly blessing me and re-writing my script.

- I was re-married to an amazing man who was studying to become a pastor

- I had a beautiful daughter and an awesome son and two cats

- Music was a very vital part of my life and so was community theatre

- I had the big blue house on the corner lot with the magnificent mountain views and a mini-van sitting in the driveway

I was so busy being angry *with* my circumstance in life, and feeling sorry for myself for all the things I had to walk through, that I FAILED to see that somehow, some way, I STILL had all those things I pictured as a little girl. As I sat there literally yelling at God, "WHY CAN'T YOU JUST GIVE ME THE DESIRES OF MY HEART? – YOU PROMISED YOU WOULD!" As God always does, he answered in that still quiet voice, "Look around you, I have given you the desires of your heart, you're just too angry to see it."

Talk about your "light bulb" moment! Hello? Anybody home? Reality knocking here!! Can I come in? I was a pastor's wife, had two children (a girl and a boy), drove a mini-van, and had the large home on the corner lot. I was a worship leader and very musical and involved in community theater. Were THESE not the pictures I had growing up? Why yes, yes they were! So why was I NOT seeing it?

I wasn't seeing it because the package in which it was delivered was not the way I envisioned it would be. I didn't acquire these things in the manner I set forth; therefore, they were void and non-existent. I focused in on all the hurt and pain of my life and all the while, God was blessing the socks off of me and I didn't see it. That's just how my God rolls! He is so awesome.

When we feel that we don't have any control in how things are going, we tend to forget who is really in control of our life. We have been given such a wonderful gift in Jesus when it comes to allowing HIM to lead us. Every day is a fresh new start and with God as the director, our "movie" can be wonderful! The beauty of a movie script is that it can be changed. Alternate endings can happen. We don't have to give up on what we once wanted for our lives. We have the option of re-writing a few scenes by the choices we make. While we can never actually "delete" a scene, we can however, learn from it and be redeemed of the poor choices that were made. Those experiences can help us write future scenes that can actually help others on their journey. What if our movie helps someone else from making the same mistakes? What a joy it is to be able to say; "I've been down that path and this is what I learned. Hopefully it helps you on your journey."

From the very beginning of the abuse, I always felt God's hand on my life. I knew He would protect me, and I knew everything would eventually be okay. After Nathan's death, I went back to my college campus to visit my friends. One of my friends pulled me aside and asked me if I was all right. At that moment, I felt a strength and peace come over me and I looked at him and said, "I am okay, I know that what I went through was for a purpose and that one day I will be able to minister to others who are walking the same path." If I had not walked through these things, I might still be that clueless person that knew no pain or hurt. It would be hard for me to relate to someone who is walking through grief from a suicide or who is in an abusive relationship if I hadn't walked through it myself. This is when you can really say; "I can empathizes with you. I've been there; I DO know how you feel."

❧Making Application in Your Life☙

What is the script like in your life? Did something or someone rewrite your dream? Are you enjoying your movie? God is a redeeming God. And although life has a way of throwing in surprises, both good and bad, we still have the ability to focus in on our blessings and the grace God gives us. When we can look past what we think is failure and see a different path that leads to the same place, we can realize that things don't always happen as we plan them, but that doesn't mean that in the end, we won't end up at the very place we long to be. Have you been too angry or hurt to see the blessings God is giving you? I challenge you to step back for a moment and try to review your life. What are some of the things you have desired? Is there any sort of resemblance of that desire being fulfilled in your life right now? Maybe it doesn't look exactly like you pictured it—but perhaps if you take your own expectations away, you might see that desire being fulfilled in a different manner. Don't allow the big things that we think are devastating overshadow all that is good. Look at the "little things", most of the time our blessings are hiding there. If you honestly can't find any blessings - then ask yourself if you are seeking the Kingdom of God first.

**"Seek ye first the kingdom of God –
and all these things shall be added unto you."**
Matthew 6:33

Chapter 19

Why Don't You Just Leave?

As a survivor of domestic violence, I realize how very blessed I am to have gotten out of the cycle of abuse. I know my story is tragic, but I also know that there are stories out there that are even more tragic than mine. One of the most commonly asked question of a domestic violence victim is, "Why don't you just leave?" *If only it were that simple.* There are so many factors that come into play when trying to answer this question. The first and foremost reason is, in my opinion, safety. Oftentimes there are threats made to the victim that if he or she tells anyone about the abuse, that the abuser will kill them. Another factor to consider is financial support. A lot of victims have small children and no financial income of their own. Sometimes staying within the abusive relationship becomes a matter of food and shelter for their family. Another reason is that victims often feel such a love connection to the abuser. They may be holding out for the abuser to change and become the person they know they can be. There are many, many factors surrounding why it's so hard for a victim to break free. But, fear has got to be the most powerful thing holding them back.

For family members or friends of a victim, there is often a sense of helplessness. They want to reach out and help more than anything. But, what they don't realize is that sometimes the help they offer could actually be putting their loved one in more danger. It is very important not to step-in and try to be the hero or rescuer without having permission from the victim. If the abuser finds out, the victim oftentimes receives another beating.

If and when the victim is ready to get out, it must be done very strategically. The best thing you can do is to let the victim know that you are there and ready to help when he or she is ready to go. Meanwhile, letting the victim know that you are there for them gives a small sense of hope. When it's safe to talk, make escape plans with the victim. Often when the time does come for the victim to leave, they leave with nothing but the clothes on their backs. Offer to store some clothing for them and the children at your house or in another location. Have the victim either give you vital and important documents such as their birth certificates, social security cards, etc. to hold on to, or encourage the victim to create a space in their existing home that is easy to get to upon exiting the home in a desperate situation. Encourage them to find those documents and put them all together in one file or envelope.

When faced yourself with the abuser in a casual or social situation, be careful not to confront him or her with what they are doing. You'll be putting yourself in danger and putting the victim in harm's way. *Imagine that conversation after they return home and are in private?*

There are all kinds of resources to help you understand and to know exactly how you can help and when you should help. I have included some facts that are listed on the Safehorizon.org website. I have also listed a few websites and phone numbers to help get you started. Please take some time and familiarize yourself with all the facts. Who knows, it might just save someone's life someday.

Chapter 20

Facts about Domestic Violence

The Victims

One in 4 women will experience domestic violence during her lifetime.

Women experience more than 4 million physical assaults and rapes because of their partners, and men are victims of nearly 3 million physical assaults.

Women are more likely to be killed by an intimate partner (30%) than men (5%).

Women ages 20 to 24 are at greatest risk of becoming victims of domestic violence.

Every year, 1 in 3 women who is a victim of homicide is murdered by her partner.

The Families

Every year, more than 3 million children witness domestic violence in their homes.

Children who live in homes where there is domestic violence are also victims of abuse or neglect in 30% to 60% of such cases.

A 2005 Michigan study found that children exposed to domestic violence at home show greater symptoms of trauma, including becoming sick more often, complaining frequently of headaches or stomachaches, and being more tired and lethargic.

A 2003 study found that children are more likely to intervene when they witness severe violence against a parent – which places the child at great risk for injury or even death.

The Circumstances

Domestic violence is most likely to occur between 6 P.M. and 6 A.M. for both female and male victims.

Domestic violence happens at home in more than 60% of reported incidents.

More domestic violence-related homicides occur in rural areas than in suburban or urban areas.

The Consequences

Among battered women living in shelters, 88% experience Post-Traumatic Stress Disorder because of domestic violence.

Among women brought to emergency rooms because of domestic violence, most were socially isolated, had lower self-esteem, and had fewer social and financial resources than other women not injured because of domestic violence.

Girls who witness domestic violence are far more likely to become victims themselves, thus continuing the cycles of victimization.

Boys who witness domestic violence are also far more likely to become abusers, of both their spouses/partners and their children, thus perpetuating the cycles of violence in their own homes.

Nearly 50% of homeless women and children are homeless because of domestic violence.

Hiding my bruises while singing in the choir

According to the U.S. Department of Housing and Urban Development, domestic violence is the third leading cause of homelessness among families.

Domestic violence costs more than $37 billion a year in law enforcement involvement, legal work, medical and mental health treatment, and lost productivity at companies.

#1 FACT

MOST CASES OF DOMESTIC VIOLENCE ARE NEVER REPORTED

*Aforementioned information was taken from the Safehorizon website. Here's the Link: http://www.safehorizon.org/index/what-we-do-2/domestic-violence--abuse-53/domestic-violence-the-facts-195.html

Chapter 21

Resources

Below are several resources that may be helpful for you or someone you know. I do not personally endorse or promote any of these web sites; but I feel they have helpful information. In the event you are faced with a life-threatening emergency, please call 911. Be sure to look up the crisis hotlines in your area.

Domestic violence
http://www.dvrc-or.org/domestic/violence/resources/C61
Or 1-866-469-8600
http://www.safehorizon.org or 1-800-621-HOPE (4673)

Teen Pregnancy/abortion
http://www.thenationalcampaign.org
http://www.teenpregnancy.com
http://www.standupgirl.com

W.I.C. (Women, infants, & children)
http://www.fns.usda.gov/wic

Cancer
http://www.cancersociety.com
http://www.cancer.org or 1-800-227-2345
http://www.cancercenter.com or 1-888-399-8121

Suicide
http://www.suicidepreventionlifeline.org or **1-800-273-TALK (8255)**
http://suicidehotlines.com ****There is a List of 1-800 numbers for each state****

Substance Abuse
 www.NIDA.NIH.gov

Alcohol Abuse (AA)
 www.aa.org